Introduc

Why are we interested in Near Death Experiences (NDE)? With the advent of the internet, social media allows masses of people to more efficiently pool together shared experiences than at any other time in history. What was once an isolated phenomenon is now a common occurrence. Whereas, in times past a simple farmer or a rich landowner who would be able to pull back from death, their story, if they chose to tell it, would be a solitary happenstance. Easily explained away or believed. It made no difference, since the significance of the account would be eventually dismissed as an outlying data point.

The recent improvement in the speed and efficiency of human communication in conjunction with modern medical methods of assisting the human body to recover after trauma has supported the explosion of accounts. And as the interpretations of each individual who returned became widely known and disseminated, others choose to finally reveal their own personal story.

Therefore a small bookshelf of NDEs is now becoming a library. Recollections from every country, culture, language and age group now reside in the great internet cloud. A mountain of data, which can no longer be wished away or ignored. The parallels and common themes from all corners of the world preclude everyone's account to be merely mass hysteria. NDEs aren't in the territory of alien encounters. Doctors, lawyers, professors, engineers, sales and service people are reporting in. Telling us similar refrains, with the added mystery of some NDEs where the person either saw or is told of events that they could not have possibly known in their current state. Taken as a whole, the only conclusion is that something must be happening, beyond our comprehension.

Hence, interested researchers are beginning to seek an explanation. For most, the objective is to prove that these are the common side effects of a brain winding down. The equivalent of a policeman telling the crowd to move on; there's nothing to see here. But, controlled experiments have a way of determining their own truth. With facts and figures, certain conclusions must be either discarded or entertained.

What Research is Telling Us

There are multiple studies underway. I know of one in the US, where pictures are placed on the ceiling of an operating room. Patients who are wheeled in, unconscious, then revived, either through direct heart stimulation or an emergency operation, then wheeled out are asked a series of questions after they come to in the recovery room. I am anxiously awaiting the results; for if they are able to identify the contents in a room where they were observed to be completely under, at all times, what more proof do you need to know that truly there is something going on.

There is one recent research that is supplying that proof. In a 2014, article in the British newspaper, The Daily Mail, we are told of a study, which spanned four years, with more than two thousand patients, all who experienced cardiac arrests. Meaning their hearts stopped and no blood was flowing through the brain, bringing oxygen and nourishment to cells anywhere in the body. Fifteen hospitals took part. The result is that almost forty percent of patients who survived told researchers about some kind of "awareness" at precisely the period when they would have been declared clinically dead.

> "Scientists at the University of Southampton conducted a four-year study of more than 2,000 patients who had suffered cardiac arrests.
>
> The research spanned cases at 15 hospitals in the UK, U.S. and Austria.
>
> The findings revealed nearly 40 per cent of those who survived described some kind of 'awareness' during the time when they were clinically dead before their hearts were restarted."[1]

Doctor Sam Parnia, who was in charge of the study tells us;

'The evidence thus far suggests that in the first few minutes after death, consciousness is not annihilated.

'Whether it fades away afterwards, we do not know, but right after death, consciousness is not lost.'

The scientists heard one man recall leaving his body entirely, watching his resuscitation from the corner of the room.

The 57-year-old social worker from Southampton was 'dead' for three minutes yet managed to recount detailed actions of the nursing staff and the sound of the machines."[2]

Why is this important? Primarily, because previous studies have demonstrated the inability of the brain to fulfill its role when the flow of blood ceases. Hence, the theory of hallucinations occurring while the brain shuts down is negated. The article has Dr. Parnia's explanation;

"Dr Parnia said: 'We know the brain can't function when the heart has stopped beating.

'But in this case conscious awareness appears to have continued for up to three minutes into the period when the heart wasn't beating, even though the brain typically shuts down within 20-30 seconds after the heart has stopped.

'This is significant, since it has often been assumed that experiences in relation to death are likely hallucinations or illusions, occurring either before the heart stops or after the heart has been successfully restarted, but not an experience corresponding with 'real' events when the heart isn't beating.

'Furthermore, the detailed recollections of visual awareness in this case were consistent with verified events.' [3]

Out of the 2,060 patients, 330 survived. Dr. Parnia reports the categories of people's experiences;

"Thirty-nine per cent of patients who survived cardiac arrest and were able to undergo interviews described a perception of awareness, but did not have any explicit memory of events.

'This suggests more people may have mental activity initially but then lose their memories after recovery, either due to the effects of brain injury or sedative drugs on memory recall,' said Dr Parnia.

Among the study participants who recalled awareness, and completed further interviews, 46 per cent experienced a wide range of mental recollections, that were not compatible with the commonly used term, near death experiences.

They included feelings of fear and persecution.

Only nine per cent had experiences commonly linked to a near death experiences, while two per cent showed full awareness or out of body experiences.

They explicitly recalled 'seeing' and 'hearing' events after their hearts had stopped.

In many of the cases, several similar trends emerged.

One in five described a feeling of peacefulness in the moment after death.

A third said time had either moved more quickly or slowed down. An out-of-body experience was felt by 13 per cent of those asked.

The bright light or golden flash image often used in Hollywood films was also described by some patients.

Others experienced a more unpleasant sensation of fears of drowning or being dragged through deep water." [4]

Dr Parnia expressed his opinion, "that the number of people having experiences when close to death would be higher were it not for drugs and sedatives given to patients."[5]

Let's look at the reported results; nine percent of the 330 had what Dr. Parnia's team would consider a NDE, while thirty-nine percent had an awareness.

I would contest the throwing out of the people included in the NDE category the people who had feelings of fear and persecution, since there are many cases reported where the NDE wasn't pleasant. Hard truths are often exposed to those who need it. Emanuel Swedenborg, the 17th century medium who wrote books about the spirit world, was allowed to be present at judgments after death and not all were pleasant.

Still with the exclusion of all any flawed experience toward the NDE tally, the percentage is higher than I would have thought. The spirit world doesn't make any near death event an occasion to communicate with us. Only those persons, who have been targeted, by reasons unexplained, are given the opportunity to converse with the other side. There is always a purpose, which may not be readily apparent for some time. This is one of the main objectives of my quest; to provide the Spiritist interpretation of the event and supply the underlying objective of the spirit realm in contacting the incarnate.

The bottom line is facts have been revealed that would have any reasonable person questioning the thesis, so loved by the illuminati of our culture today, that we are just organic animals, destined to rot away, without a soul, without a purpose in life, other than to consume.

The Real Reason Why We are Interested in NDEs

Which brings me to the second point of why many of us are fascinated with NDEs; the first being the appearance of data and its analysis, the second, the true underlying cause, is the emptiness of our spiritual side.

We know, in our hearts and in the deep recesses of our mind, that we are not mere animals, surviving for a few moments of time on the planet. Why else would so many seek an explanation for this longing. This feeling that there is a higher cause, a purpose for our life.

V

The study of NDEs reveals a common theme. We are not just shells with a brain, wired to survive and reproduce to spread our genes far and wide. We are on earth for a reason; to improve and one day become a pure spirit. In that short sentence lie volumes of unanswered questions, gratefully we have received some guidance. Revelations from Allan Kardec, Francisco (Chico) Xavier, and others, supplies us the foundation of knowledge that are now available to us to research in order to take various NDEs and translate the underlying reasons for the NDE, the context of the messages being delivered to the recipient and an explanation of the other world seen through human eyes.

When you read the recollections by the individuals who experienced their time in a different dimension, communicating with beings from the earliest myths of the human race to named spirits in the Bible, you only read one side of the story. The chronicler witness's events and sights that are completely foreign with no baseline of human experience which prepares them to fully comprehend the significance of what swirls around during those precious moments in the spiritual world.

The Doctrine of Spiritism provides the commentary to fill in the blanks, to explain the processes whereby souls are taken, shown fantastic displays and imparted information. Not all details are known, but using the compass of Spiritist teachings, light is shone upon the questions we all have:

1. Why is the spirit world communicating to us?

2. Are we truly given specific tasks to perform while on earth?

3. Why are we loved to such a degree as described by near death survivors?

4. How can we see past family members?

5. Have we all lived before?

6. How are we judged and why?

7. How can the spirit world show us the future and different scenarios of the future, one where we are on earth and one where we alter the lives of all who were affected by our presence?

8. How are we guided by the spirit world?

Only by understanding the broader vision of the spirit world, can we focus our energies on what we are on earth for; bettering ourselves. We need to cast off the anchors of excessive materialism, free the ties to earth and establish a path to ascend. To rise to the level we desire to attain.

A herald has appeared, not just one, but each person who has written about their incident. They are telling us to wake up and look around. Life is more than the accumulation of goods; it is about love and caring for your family, your neighbors and beyond. It is about being an honest and civically involved person. It is about studying to accumulate what is expected of us and analyzing our trials on earth so we may determine how to pass the tests that life presents.

This book is your pathway to unlock the mysteries of the spirit world. It is just a beginning step, but a required one. By reading and understanding what others have seen, you will determine for yourself the extent of the love and guidance that constantly surrounds every human on earth and assists you to make the choice to place your first foot toward the journey to purify your soul.

What Really Happens During Near Death Experiences, According to Spiritism

What Really Happens During Near Death Experiences, According to Spiritism

12 NDE's Explained and Explored

By

Brian Foster

http://www.nwspiritism.com/

1st Edition

Volume 1

Table of Contents

Introduction i

    What Research is Telling Us ii

    The Real Reason Why We are Interested in NDEs v

What Really Happens During Near Death Experiences, According to Spiritism viii

Table of Contents ix

Chapter 1 – The Intersection of NDEs and Spiritism..................12

    What is Spiritism? 14

    The View from the Other Side 15

Chapter 2 - NDE – James' Life Review 19

    James' Life Review 19

    On Earth to Improve 21

    Pre-Planning for Events in Our Life....................................22

Chapter 3 – NDE – Alternate Futures for Michael.....................25

    The Accident...25

    A Future with Michael Alive 27

    Visions of Heavens and Hell 28

    How God Sees Us 30

Chapter 4 - Howard Storm's NDE Descent into Purgatory 32

    The Spirit World – the Good and the Bad............................33

    Howard's Death 35

    The Lower Zone...36

    Howard's Escape 38

    Howard's Review of his Life...40

    Howard's Ascent 42

    The Return..43

Chapter 5 – What is the Doctrine of Spiritism 45

    Jesus promised us more Information 45

    What is Spiritism? 46

Chapter 6- Other Death Experience – Nicola and the son of her friend...49

    The Extraordinary Occurrence 50

    Proof of a Life Plan 53

Chapter 7 – NDE - Anna Discovers her Mission 57

    The Ascent into the Light 57

Anna's New Body 58
Meeting her Family 60
Anna's Job 61
Anna Learns About the Importance of her Work 62
Conclusion 63
Chapter 8 - ADC – After Death Communication – David G. 64
The Death of his Niece 64
David's New Calling 68
Chapter 9 – NDE - William H Detects the Universal Intelligence 70
The Over Soul 70
Feelings of Love 72
Chapter 10 - NDE - Sara Finds Out How we are Assisted by the Spirit World 74
Sara's Accident 77
The Transformation 78
The Result 81
Chapter 11 – NDE - Amy - A Young Woman who May Have Attempted Suicide 86
The Cause of Amy's NDE 86
In the Room 87
Amy Leaves the Room 94
Amy Learns About the Universe 97
Amy Learns About the True Extent of Our Lives 98
Amy Learns About Herself 100
Amy Returns 102
One More Coincidence 105
Chapter 12 - Bronwen's Two NDE's and the Plan for her Life ..107
Her First Experience 107
Her Second Experience 108
Searching for Her Task 109
New Attitude toward Religion 112
Chapter 13 – NDE - Ronnie - The boy who was ran over by a car 116
The Story 116
The Accident 117
At the Hospital 118
A Miracle? 120
What Probably Did Happen? 122
X

Ronnie's Experience in the Other World..............................124
Chapter 14 – NDE – Romy - The Car Accident which Triggered
Perfect Recall..127
The Reassuring Voice...127
The Memory Bank...128
An Application of a Recording...131
What Romy Learned 133
Chapter 15 – Final Thoughts 135
Your Exploration Continues 137
The Case for Reincarnation – Your Path to Perfection 139
Spiritism 101 –The Third Revelation 142
7 Tenets of Spiritism – How They Impact Your Daily Life....144
Explore Your Destiny – Since Your Life's Path is (mostly)
Predetermined...146
Author...149
Copyright...150
Bibliography 151

Chapter 1 – The Intersection of NDEs and Spiritism

In the United States there has been literature and research about NDEs (near death experiences) for quite a few years now. There are many stories on the internet detailing what occurs for people that have had a NDE. The stories could have been lifted from one of the many books psychographed by Francisco C. Xavier. Xavier is a follower of Spiritism, which has been around since the 1850's, founded by Allan Kardec. Spiritism is able to put NDE's in context and explains in full what other people, through their experiences, have started to explore.

There has been numerous stories about NDEs (Near Death Experiences) since mankind have been on earth, but with the advent of the internet, the gathering and discussion of people's experiences has reached a new level. To the people visiting and writing about NDEs, their conception of the order of the Universe and their place within it have undergone a transformation. The knowledge that they really have a soul and it lives beyond their physical body brings a whole new set of questions. These questions can be answered by Spiritism.

Some of the recent NDE stories published on the nderf.org (Near Death Experience Research Foundation) site, underline the sense of otherworldliness and provides motivation to explore the state of the universe in which our spirit lives.

"While I was on the stretcher I observed a very white light at a distance, which I was approaching, I was like floating in the air." writes Victorio from Argentina, published in March, 2014.[6] He goes on to describe;

> "This unfolding of pictures and gaps developed and progressed continuously, presenting a constant delicate consequential line in perfect order, a chain of events, yet somehow they were all happening at once. The past the present and the future were all happening at once. It was inspiring to witness the order and

sense that all these little pictures seemed to have in "the big picture". I felt a lot of compassion. I was all forgiven. In fact there was nothing to forgive. I could see that my life had "perfect order" to it. In some way it was like watching a mathematical equation or sum that makes perfect sense- such event and such event create this kind of result. It was a simple portrayal of natural cause and effect with a gentle understanding."[7]

People experiencing NDEs write about meeting spirits and communicating with deceased family members, as Fabio, from Italy, "I 'feel' a presence, something, someone, I can't explain it. I saw nothing and heard no word, nevertheless, I suddenly realize that the 'speaker' had always been there, and had followed me while I was in the tunnel, and somehow he had perhaps helped me to turn back. We began a silent dialogue. An immense and unconditional love. A flow of love."[8]

Who are these other beings and how can we talk with family members long gone from the earth? Does our spirit only live once in a physical body or do we truly travel through multiple lives? Many religions and individuals believe in the concept of reincarnation. Reincarnation provides a framework for the existence of an immortal soul and a reason why we are truly reborn. People, who had no religious beliefs before, upon reviving from NDEs have returned accepting their soul to be immortal and that reincarnation is a necessary process for our quest to become a better and more loving individual.

Kevin Williams, who works on the www.near-death.com website, has complied and quoted parts of a research paper by Amber Wells, in his article he highlights to following:

"The majority of experiencers mentioned learning or enlightenment as the main purpose underlying reincarnation. Here are some comments by experiencers:

"The spirit needs to embody itself in matter to

13

experience it and learn. There are karmic patterns to learn lessons and to work spirit in matter."

"Life itself is a series of learnings. The lessons are universal, the two most important being truth and forgiveness."

"We progress at our own rate to reach the light. If you do things that take you away from the light, then you are perpetuating your time here."

"The inner quality is there, the inner self remains, but the external aspect that may have seemed very strong is dissolved. Individuality wasn't the same there. It was the same as everybody and everybody was me. Your spirit is always you. You are not the personality that you are on Earth. In the other realm you are everything, light is everything."[9]

The findings and comments above are all explained by the doctrines of Spiritism. The people who have traveled through a NDE knew what they experienced, but now they have a name for the entire construct of the universe in which they entered for that brief period of time.

What is Spiritism?

Spiritism explains why we are here on earth, the causes of why we must live through good and bad times, and provides the basis behind the reasons why we travel through successive lives. Spiritism was presented to us by the spirit world so we here on earth may perfect ourselves to prepare the earth to reach a higher plane of existence, while at the same time to improve our capacity to love one another.

The View from the Other Side

The view of our experiences from the spirit world can be discovered in the books by Allan Kardec and Chico Xavier. Allan Kardec, in his book *The Spirits Book*, documents, by a series of questions and answers, what happens during the separation of the body and the soul:

154. *Is the separation of the soul from the body a painful process?*

"No; the body often suffers more during life that at the moment of death, when the soul is usually unconscious of what is occurring to the body. The sensations experienced at the moment of death are often a source of enjoyment for the spirit, who recognizes them as putting an end to the term of his exile."

155. *How is the separation of soul and body effected?*

"The bonds which retained the soul being broken, it disengages itself from the body."

Is this separation effected instantaneously, and by means of an abrupt transition? Is there any distinctly marked line of demarcation between life and death?

"No; the soul disengages itself gradually. It does not escape at once from the body, like a bird whose cage is suddenly opened. The two states touch and run into each other; and the spirit extricates himself, little by little, from his fleshly bonds, which are loosed, but not broken." [10]

These statements were written in the 1850's, well before the formal documentation of NDEs arrived. Doesn't the above fit perfectly with the sensation of the spirit somewhat free of the body, communicating with and seeing other spirits, but still connected? All who have had a NDE still had had a bond with their body, otherwise they would not have been able to return to their physical form. Death is only the destruction of our body, our soul is immortal.

In Allan Kardec's book, *Heaven and Hell*, an evocation is being held at a Mortuary chamber on April 23, 1862. The participants are communicating with Mr. Sanson, who was a member of the Parisian Spiritist Society, he died on April 21, 1862. He had spent a year in suffering before his death and he expressed the wish to be communicated with after his death. Here are some of the excerpts:

7. *Did you retain your awareness up to the last instant?*

"Yes, my spirit retained its faculties. I no longer saw; I foresaw. My entire life unfolded within my memory and my last remembrance, my dying request, was to be able to communicate with you as I am doing right now. I next asked God to watch over you so that the dream of my life could be fulfilled."

8. *Were you conscious at the moment in which your body breathed its last? What happened to you at that time? What sensations did you feel?*

"Life expires and sight, or rather, the spirit's sight darkens. You find yourself in the void, the unknown, and then as if carried by an unknown power, you find yourself in a world where all is joy and wonder. I no longer felt anything, nor was I sure about what was occurring: nevertheless, an ineffable happiness surrounded me and I no longer felt the grip of pain."[11]

Again, the same sensations, the same feelings of love and joy. There is a book, *Workers of the Life Eternal*, which was dictated to Chico Xavier in 1946, by the spirit Andre Luiz, which describes a death experience from the point of view of one of the spirit helpers in facilitating a person's passing over to the spirit world. Andre was assigned to a team of spirits who are to assist a man named Dimas to complete his life. Dimas' mother, is also there in spirit to help her son in his first moments back in the spirit realm. The chapter on Dimas tells of the spirit helpers preparing him for the final transition:

> "Dimas-discarnate was now hovering a few inches above Dimas-corpse, attached to his body only by a thin, silvery cord similar to a delicate elastic thread between the abandoned brain of dense matter and the brain of rarefied matter of the liberated organism.
>
> Dimas' mother quickly left the material body and gathered up the new form, wrapping it in a pure white tunic that she had brought with her.
>
> To our incarnate friends, Dimas was completely dead. To us, though, the operation was not yet complete. The Assistant determined that the fluidic cord should remain intact until the following day, taking into account the needs of the "dead man", who was not yet fully prepared for a quicker disengagement.
>
> And while the doctor was providing technical explanations to the sobbing relatives, Jeronimo invited us to leave, while entrusting the newly discarnate soul to the care of the woman who had been his devoted mother in the physical world."[12]

The act of dying is not a solitary experience, but one in which the spirit world actively assist us. The writings of the spirit domain reinforces and provides an independent validation of the findings of the research into NDE experiences. In fact, Spiritism provides the context, the reason, and the motivation for our life here on earth.

As one can see, the statements presented in Amber Well's paper, such as, "Life itself is a series of learnings. The lessons are universal, the two most important being truth and forgiveness", have also been delivered to us via an alternative channel. That of the spirit world communicating directly to mediums to alert us of a life beyond our single human existence.

In a later Chapter we shall explain the Doctrine of Spiritism in greater detail.

Chapter 2 - NDE – James' Life Review

James had a full life review, with a council determining if he should stay or return. He also found out that indeed, he did have a life plan.

James had major surgery. During his operation his heart stopped and he was guided to the spirit world. There, he was brought in front of a tribunal, to determine if he should return or not to his physical life.

You can read his whole story at the **NHNE Near Death** website.

James' Life Review

When James' heart stopped, a woman spirit approached him and led him out of our world to the spirit world. Where, as many others before him have noted, the flowers and trees shined as if lit from within. In the books psychographed by Francisco C. Xavier, the spirits who communicate with us, also comment about the wondrous aspects of the light, how their senses are heighten and everything takes on a brilliant hue, with colors that we have never seen before.

James then describes where his life would be reviewed:

"I was led by the lady through the forest. I asked where we were, what had happened to me, where were we going. I was told everything was fine and my questions would be answered soon. I didn't feel concerned in fact I felt calm and Peaceful. I was led by the lady to a clearing in the forest in the middle of which was a large wooded oval table with 10 or 11 people seated around it and one chair empty which I was indicated to sit at. Then the lady left. The people at the table seemed very familiar, but in an 'other' worldly way and also had the same young but old looking qualities. I was warmly welcomed and told that I had left my physical body, and the purpose of the council was to decide if I should stay or return to it, and that a review would take place to determine this. The review consisted of a screen which appeared above the table in the center which began to play a 'film' of my life from the moment I was born. Members of the council paused the film at different parts and we looked at the circumstances surrounding specific events, sometimes from the different perspectives of the other people involved, but mostly they were interested in how the experiences had affected me, and my feelings about things." [13]

In the spirit world, as on earth, we all have our group of friends. Friends who have been with us since we were in school and who have always been concerned with our welfare; constantly checking on our progress, with the noble aim of assisting us in our major life challenges. We have our friends in the spirit world, who are all the more special because they sometimes watch over us and other times they reincarnate to share our trials together.

Additionally, we all have mentors, older and wiser people who we look for advice and guidance. Again, the same concept applies to our spiritual mentors. The group that worked with James is most probably made up of friends and mentors, souls that he has intimately known in his spirit life, but due to his recent separation from his body, his memory before the commencement of his current physical life is hazy. Hence, he seems to know them and feels comfortable in their presence.

Next, James' life is reviewed. And not just his actions, but the emotional affect he had upon others and the motivations that caused his actions are analyzed. This is one of the central tenets of Spiritism, our thoughts are actions, for with thoughts all begins and actions are merely the completion of a thought.

It gets more complex, for our very thoughts influence events and others around us. We are all like radio towers, beaming our innermost musings and emotional highs and lows to those around us. The spirit world tells us we have a responsibility to control the waves emanating from our brains.

This all sounds extremely difficult to perform, but think for a moment, why this must be so. As we progress and become higher and pure spirits, the power of our minds also increase in force.

Therefore, to ascend in the ranks of the spirits, we must learn to control that which shall, in the future, possess great power.

James then tells us about the analysis of his life to date:

"The experience was uncomfortable at times, I had to see myself warts and all, I saw the best and the worst in myself. But never at any time did I feel I was being judged by anyone present. We reached my present circumstances and I saw that my lung condition had been created by myself to give me an exit opportunity. We had a long debate after the film about my life blueprint and whether or not I had fulfilled my chosen experiences which were mostly linked to previous lifetimes and spiritual 'baggage' that needed to be cleared and healed. I felt that I needed more time on earth and this was agreed by the council, who also told me that I would need to go back more spiritually awake to accomplish this."[14]

On Earth to Improve

James understands completely the reason for his life on earth when he writes the words, "life blueprint". First, this proves that James is an advanced spirit, for spirits that exist on the lower planes, who aren't interested in improving themselves, are arbitrarily assigned their station, appearance and trials in life.

While those who are actively attempting to overcome the deficiencies they detected in their last sojourn on the planet, focus on repairing those holes in their next life and participate in laying out the plan for their time on earth in great detail.

There are many instances of this in Spiritist literature. One example is of a man who committed suicide in a previous life, abandoning his wife and children to destitution, and is planning his next life. In the book, *Memoirs of a Suicide*, he tells of his "blueprint":

"I won't be able to have children! By not looking after my family; by rejecting, half way through, the honorable responsibility of being head of the household in order to help me ascend in merit. I put myself in the wretched position of not being granted the chance of building a family and being a father again in my next existence!"[15]

Hence, James is but one example of a person planning to overcome what they failed in their previous life. Therefore, the trials that we select, or to put it in a different manner, the classes in the school of earth that we register for, are all required prerequisites in our quest to become higher spirits. At some point in the future, we will attain that goal and no longer need to wear our earthly clothes.

Pre-Planning for Events in Our Life

Another fascinating comment made by James is his mentioning that his lung condition was pre-planned. How can that be? Well, again, this is not uncommon in the spiritual world.

Not only do we determine the complete diagram of our bodies, but we also plan in advance afflictions that await us. In the book, *Missionaries of the Light*, by Francisco C. Xavier, inspired by the spirit Andre Luiz, Andre talks to a spirit who works in the Reincarnation Planning Center in the heavenly city Nosso Lar. He points out the extent of our future planning:

> "Here is the plan for the future reincarnation of a friend of mine. Do you see some dark spots from the descending colon to the sigmoid loop? This indicates that he will suffer from a large ulcer in this area as soon as he becomes an adult. Nevertheless, he has chosen it."[16]

The extent of the details that are invested in planning for our corporeal experiences is truly astonishing. Therefore, no one should take their life lightly, for countless hours of dedication were devoted to preparing our entry into our campus called Earth.

James recovered from his operation and returned to the land of the living, but he was a changed man. He trained as a Hypnotherapist and became a Past Life Therapist, focusing on the time spans between physical existences. As was determined by the council that judged him, he was given increased spiritual powers, which enabled him to begin assisting others in their own spiritual awakening.

James talks about his increased sensitivity:

"After my NDE, and once I was working with myself spiritually I started having out of body experiences. At first I would 'awake' from sleep to find myself watching myself sleep! then I began to leave my body and go to the spirit realms where I met my spirit guides and also people I have known who have passed from the earth; my grandparents, people who I had cared for in my work. My spirit guides began to 'educate' me about the different states of existence that a soul passes through in its great journey through creation, and also to show me things that would come to pass on the earth, how the earth would change and become less dense than it is now."[17]

All of James' NDE is explained and given context by the Doctrine of Spiritism. Spiritism reveals to us that we are all immortal spirits, striving to improve; that we must control our selfish and materialistic tendencies to be more loving, fraternal and spiritual. We are on earth to help others also ascend.

The spirit world is the real world, where our family resides. Families that have been reincarnated in different permutations through multiple generations. Always at our sides and constantly reaching out to be of assistance.

Spiritism is guiding the entire human race to a better place. As written in the books by Allan Kardec, the codifier of Spiritism; the earth will change. Currently, the earth is a planet of atonement, where immature spirits live to learn and to pay for their past mistakes.

In the future, the earth will be a planet of regeneration, where there will be more good souls than bad and selfishness, jealousy, and wars are a thing of the past. Our bodies will become lighter, for as our spirits advance our ties to the physical world become less dense; hence our temporary human casings no longer require physical brute force to survive in a savage world.

Chapter 3 – NDE – Alternate Futures for Michael

Michael J had one of the most complete NDE's that I have seen. He was able to retain many memories from his experience. His revelations of the spirit world are fascinating. I take the reader through Michael's experiences and relate what the spirit world is actually doing.

Michael J, as a result of a terrible accident when he was a young man, had an extensive NDE experience. He talked to the spirits, looked at alternative futures and was told of upcoming events. You can read his whole story at the NDERF.org website.

The Accident

Michael was climbing on limestone cliffs on a frozen day, when part of the boulder he was hanging onto suddenly broke free. He and the large rock both fell, with the boulder landing on top of him. According to Michael's recollection, the stone weighed 400-500 pounds. He felt that he left his body and seeing himself, he knew he was dead. Next Michael encounters a spirit guide:

"He told me this was an accident and I <could> go back, IF I wanted. I told him by my thoughts there was no way to make that body work. It was squashed flat. He basically told me that he could make it work again. Did I want to go back? I wanted to know my options. What would happen if I chose to go back and what would happen if I didn't. No sooner did I think these thoughts and BOOM, I was hit with a package of images. It showed in brief what would happen if I didn't go back. I saw my sister get into alcohol and drugs and her life spin out of control ... BECAUSE I wasn't there. I saw my Dad commit suicide because of my death shortly after my mom divorced him over the matter of my death. I saw my paternal grandfather wither away and die, his heart broken over my death and my dad's suicide. There were twin blows that destroyed all the joy he had left in life. The effects went on and on, my mom was sad and heart broken the rest of her life and so very lonely ... And I saw a parade of faces of people I would never meet and whose lives I would have impacted and whose lives would have impacted mine but now I would never know any of them and they would never know me. The man in the white robe had me with my sister. I've always loved my little sister and for her alone I would have chosen to come back but seeing all that pain it would cause everyone else ... mom, dad, grandparents, friends, cousins, aunts, uncles ... man I HAD to go back." [18]

Michael's spirit guide, or guardian angel as many people call it, was right there in an instant. People who have had NDEs recognize that we live close to the spirit world. They are all around us, watching, guiding and trying to lead us to become better souls. But for most of us, the thought that spirits, or worse ghosts, inhabit the same space is a primitive notion and should be discarded, otherwise we would demonstrate to the world our ignorance and naivety. What if, these uncivilized people, who lived closer to nature and by no choice of their own, possessed little material goods, detected a truth about our sphere and the spirit realm that we have lost? Could we, who must be presented with absolute proof of everything, be missing something important, right before our eyes?

An alternative future was shown to Michael. How could this be? Allan Kardec, in his *The Spirits Book*, describes the power of a high spirit. He likens it to us, here on earth, walking through a trail in a canyon, not knowing what the next bend will look like. Whereas, the spirit, sitting on the mountain top, sees our path, where it will lead and other paths that may be offered to us. Still, this is easy to say, but how could this be in practice? What type of instantaneous mathematical calculations of probability, combined with moving pictures of those possibilities must be processed to present in a life like simulation a series of future options? I have no clue, but imagining how this could be done, may be a worthwhile pursuit.

A Future with Michael Alive

Next, Michael was shown what would happen if he chose to return to his physical body:

> "Then came a second package of images, those of what would happen IF I went back. I skipped over the obvious. Dad DIDN'T commit suicide. My sister turned out Ok. Mom ended up happy. My grandfather went on to beam with pride over his first grandson to attend a university. My grandfather was a legal immigrant from Italy who never made it past the 4th grade and he treasured education beyond EVERYTHING. He crowed like a proud rooster when his kids graduated from high school and I became the first of his grandkids to attend a prestigious university. But what I focused on in this second package was what I would pay as a price for going back. I knew that I would walk again, that all I had lost would be restored but only temporarily. In my latter life, perhaps 10 to 15 years after the accident, I would suffer pain, extreme pain and it would affect me the rest of my life.

> I chose to come back. He smiled, as if he KNEW I would pick the harder path because of how I felt for my family and friends. There was a snap and a pop and I was back in my body. It was FILLED with crackling electricity like sounds and feelings. I had no breath, no air and this huge rock was choking off all air. I grabbed the small end of the tear near my nose with my one free left hand (my right arm was pinned under the rock) and rolled the thing off me like it was made of paper mache`."[19]

Michael's perispirit, the connection we have from our spirit to our physical bodies, was re-attached to his broken body. From the second option presented, one can see how positive influences have far-reaching and significant effects on other people's lives. We should never underestimate our power to help. While things may appear to us to be small and unimportant, one never knows how our action could be translated into helping or harming another person's life and the relations of that person.

Visions of Heavens and Hell

Michael was next transported to the hospital, where he experienced his second phase of the NDE:

> "The next thing I know I'm back in the operating room where the surgeon is working frantically to save my life and as he works at massaging my heart I found myself drifting away and the further I drifted the darker the room got and the further away his voice sounded, Found myself well above the operating theater where I should have been on a floor above that room or outside looking on a roof, but I wasn't. Instead I was floating in the entrance to a tunnel or vortex. I was sucked into it and then was when my adventure REALLY began.
>
> I ended up with a life review, and was escorted around "the other side" by a being who was my guardian angel/teacher whom I came to call "professor" but he had an incredible sense of humor. I say "he" with tongue in cheek because "he" was neither a he or a she.
>
> I saw what happened to true atheists (apparently I was opened minded enough that I didn't qualify). I got to see various "heavens" and asked to see what "Hell" was like if there was one (and there was but it was nothing like I expected). I even asked to meet Jesus and apologize only to meet a man that was nothing like I expected and was given interesting historical facts I was later able to verify.
>
> But all of that is FAR TOO complex to include here, including numerous predictions of the future that have ALL come true except ONE, which I think is yet to happen"[20]

Michael's guardian angel gave him the complete tour. Michael was gifted with a life review, so in the future; he would know what type of actions stand out, in either good or bad light. People with NDEs are extremely lucky to have the opportunity to have their tests graded before the end of their allotted time, so they can improve in the second half of their exam.

According to various books, psychographed by Francisco C. Xavier, and inspired by the spirit Andre Luiz, when true atheists die, meaning those who absolutely expect to never wake up again, they don't wake up. They exist in a sleep-like state, since our thoughts are our actions in the spirit world. Only with time and assistance from helpful spirits, are these souls stirred to life, and made ready for their time in the spirit world.

Michael's description of various heavens is correct. There are different levels of heavens. There are celestial cities around our planet awaiting good souls to ascend. Additionally, as we become purer spirits, there are places reserved for various levels of spirits. In fact, the whole universe is filled with colonies of spirits, each one, according to the Law of Affinity (whereby spirits who have attained similar inclinations gather together).

As to Hell, Michael may have one of the locations where spirits who have committed crimes are assembled, again caused by the Law of Affinity. I have heard one of these places described as appearing like an Asian city about 150 years ago, somewhat dirty, slaves pulling carts, and the feeling of violence in the air.

An alternative site that may have been shown to Michael could have been the Lower Zone, where spirits, who are tied to earth, still wander. The Lower Zone starts right on the surface of our planet and ascends some miles upwards, until it hits the border of the celestial cities. Now you may say, this is impossible, I look up and see nothing but sky. We cannot detect these places because they exist in a different place or dimension than us. Remember, spirits are less dense and composed of energy, while we are composed of matter.

As mentioned earlier, higher level spirits have knowledge of the future and Michael was told of certain events that would happen, and they did. All foretold events, except one, which may occur in the future, have transpired. Others may read this and think, just coincidences, Michael's brain was shutting down and somehow he thought images in his mind told him all that he wrote. But ask yourself, how could he have known the future? Yes, he

29

could have, in his imagination, visited heaven, have conversations with spirits, experienced many other sensations, but he was given concrete happenings.

Another interesting comment was made by Michael in his report. At the end of the description of a NDE, there is a series of questions posed to the person who is reporting the event.

> **"At what time during the experience were you at your highest level of consciousness and alertness?** After I was clear of my body, BOTH times. As I said before, I have an IQ of about 150, genius level and yet when out of my body, in a "dead" state, I found myself WAY smarter. Comparing the two. I'd consider myself a drooling moron to what I was outside my limiting body."[21]

When you are pure energy, think of the power of your mind. Think of what you know now and realize that you know nothing. Think of the so-called real-world people say you should acknowledge and think to yourself; that they have no clue about the real reality. We are but a physical speck of dust, on earth to learn the correct attitudes so the vast resources of our intellectual ability can be put to good use.

How God Sees Us

Lastly, Michael gives an answer to one of the questions, which I believe illustrates how we all connect and how God hears our prayers and sees all:

> **"During your experience, did you encounter any specific information / awareness that a mystical universal connection or unity/oneness either does (or does not) exist?** Yes   I EXPERIENCED that universal connection. We are both part of a great supernatural "internet" and yet simultaneously separate PCs as well (to use an analogy)."[22]

In the book, In the Realms of Mediumship, psychographed by Francisco C. Xavier and inspired by the spirit Emmanuel, the Preface of the book written by Emmanuel, tells us;

30

"Through the sentiments that characterize their inner life, all individuals emit specific rays and live within the spiritual wave with which they identify themselves.

Such truths cannot remain semi-hidden in our sanctuaries of faith; they will radiate from the temples of science like mathematical equations."[23]

Hence, Michael is describing the concept of the Internet, where we all have a unique identifier and we are in constant communication with all around us. Our minds are continually transmitting information which the spirit world receives. Our waking conscious may not be able to decipher the code, although some people have fleeting moments of intuition that make it through our physical filters.

In summary, Michael's NDE substantiates, independently of the Doctrine of Spiritism, the complex and overwhelming power of the hidden world around us. The Druids called it the "Other World", for they too knew that we are but temporary casings housing an immortal soul.

Chapter 4 - Howard Storm's NDE Descent into Purgatory

Howard Storm was an atheist professor who had a NDE where he visited hell and came out a changed man. This affected him so much, he wrote a book about his experience. His book is called, *My Descent into Death*, the link to his book on Amazon is in the title. The book was discussed on the website, blog.godreports.com, the title of the story is, *Atheist professor's near-death experience in hell left him changed*, by Mark Ellis.

Howard describes himself;

"I was a double atheist," says Howard Storm, who became a tenured art professor at Northern Kentucky University by age 27. "I was a know-it-all college professor, and universities are some of the most closed-minded places there are," he notes.[24]

I have heard stories like Howard's before. At an IANDS (International Association for Near-Death Studies) conference. A young woman in her late teens, arrogant, sure of herself and full of disdain for others, who was in a car crash and experienced her NDE as the car was turning in slow motion just about to be broadsided by an on-coming speeding car.

She wasn't first visited by angelic spirits, instead a sinister orb materialized next to her. Then transformed into a dwarf-like creature with a sinister voice. He told her that she had screwed up her whole life and belonged with him, beneath the earth. She resisted and then other inferior spirits tried to talk her into descending. When she continued to resist, they hurled all types of insults toward her.

Only when, in her mind, she cried for divine help, did her spirit guide answer and lead her on a journey of her life and its possibilities.

Hence, when I saw Howard's story I was intrigued. Recollections of people who are exposed to the lower realms of inferior spirits and evil reveal the extent of the spirit world to us, just as importantly as when people visit heavenly apparitions.

The Spirit World – the Good and the Bad

As much as we would like to believe in the possibility of complete forgiveness for all of our sins without penalty, the evidence is against it. Yes, God is love and will always love us, even when we commit crimes and fail in our life. Eternal love from God and Jesus is a certainty. But we must remember we are loved as we love our children. Children must learn the hard way sometimes. They must understand that in the near future they will have to pay for their mistakes. Hence, while love that rains down upon our off-spring is constant, we allow adversity do its part to teach our children about life, so one day they may grow up to be outstanding citizens and aware of the rules of the world. Therefore, yes, we are forgiven, but we still have to account for our wrongs.

First, let's explore what are spirits. In *The Spirits Book*, by Allan Kardec, which is a compilation of questions that Allan Kardec posed to mediums around Europe to gain answers to questions that concern the meaning of our lives and the universe, there is a description of a spirit:

76. *What definition can be given of spirits?*

"Spirits may be defined as the intelligent beings of the creation. They constitute the population of the universe, in contradistinction to the forms of the material world."[25]

We are spirits and we are immortal. We travel through successive lives in order to improve ourselves. Some of us are more advanced than others and unfortunately some spirits are caught in the lower zones by their selfish and off-times criminal attitudes and behavior.

We on earth swim in the same ocean as the lower spirits, they are all around us, interacting and watching our lives. Our guardian angels are with us too. All of this is for a purpose, so we may grow in our ability to resist bad temptations. No difference than when

33

most of us were in high school and we lived in a closed society with good and upright students, arrogant and exclusive students, and amongst the drug dealers and petty thieves. We soon congregated into our natural groups, those friends where we shared bonds of affinity.

The Divine Law of Affinity, which at our early stage in our progress toward perfection is the great selector. By it, we are divided into which type of group we shall be reborn, where we go when we die, and what are the characteristics of the next level we strive for. The Law states that souls with certain attributes, attitudes, beliefs and values are associated with like-minded spirits.

We are all created the same at the starting point. Then we are given the opportunity to climb the ladder. *The Spirits Book* clues us in on the process:

115. *Are some spirits created good and others created bad?*

"God has created all spirits in a state of simplicity and ignorance, that is to say, without knowledge. He has given to each of them a mission, with a view to enlighten them and to make them gradually arrive at perfection through the knowledge of the truth, and thus to bring them nearer and nearer to himself. This perfection is, for them, the condition of eternal and unalloyed happiness. Spirits acquire knowledge by passing through the trials imposed on them by God. Some of them accept these trials with submission, and arrive more quickly at the aim of their destiny others undergo them with murmuring, and thus remain, through their own fault, at a distance from the perfection and the felicity promised to them."[26]

Hence, all of us have begun as primitive beings, where might makes right and we take what we can get. Eventually we grow out of that mindset and it is replaced by the acknowledgement that love, charity and fraternity is the correct path.

All of the discussion above is a prelude to understanding what really happened to Howard and who is doing it to him. For without comprehending the rules of the earth's sphere of influence and determining who is around us and why they act in the manner they do is imperative to not only grasp the meaning of Howard's experience but of our own as well.

Howard's Death

Howard fell ill with a perforated intestine in France. He was only thirty-eight years old. Since it was a Saturday, the French government hospital couldn't find a doctor to perform surgery. Howard had to wait until the next day to be seen. Meanwhile, his body was being poisoned by the fluids leaking from his intestines into his stomach cavity. He said his farewells to his wife and prepared to die.

Mark Ellis, in his article wrote what happen to Howard next:

"It wasn't long after he lost consciousness that he had a very unusual out-of-body experience, and found himself standing next to his bed, looking at himself lying there. As he stood there, he noticed he didn't feel the pain in his stomach. He felt more alive than ever, and his senses seemed more heightened than usual.

He tried to communicate with his wife and another man in the room, but they didn't respond, which frustrated him. "I was glad I didn't have the pain, but also I was very confused and disturbed by the situation."

'I saw my body lying on the bed, but I refused to believe it was me. How could that be me if I was standing there,' he wondered."[27]

Howard's spirit had separated from his body. In his spirit form he left behind earthly pain. Unbeknownst to Howard, he was still connected to his body by a slim, almost invisible silvery cord. Similar in function to the umbilical cord, this cord attaches the spirit to the body, via the perispirit.

When we are reborn, our perispirit covers the entire body like a transparent wet suit. It enables communication between our spirit and our body. Once the perispirit is cut from the body that is when physical life is truly over. When the link is severed, the dense suit specially made for our journey on earth is left to rot and recycle.

Howard wasn't met by his celestial spirit guides or past members of his family as others have experienced in their NDEs. A group of inferior spirits, who knew in advance of his coming were there to meet him. Speaking English, which surprised Howard, since he was in a French hospital, they gave him orders to follow:

"Come with us," they said. "Hurry up, let's go."

Howard went to the doorway. "Are you from the doctor?" he asked. "I need to have surgery. I'm sick and I've been waiting a long time."

"We know all about you," one said. "We've been waiting for you. It's time for you to go. Hurry up."[28]

"We know all about you", isn't that a strange, yet terrifying statement to hear upon your death? How did they know all about him? The answer is they have been watching him for a long time. Spirits in the Lower Zone (a purgatory, a temporary location where errant spirits are given time to readjust their beliefs and attitudes) are constantly on the lookout to recruit their own kind. They were attracted to Howard through the Law of Affinity. They felt, by analyzing his thoughts and actions, that he would be a prime candidate to join their group.

The Lower Zone

What is the Lower Zone? Andre Luiz, who woke up there after his death on the operating room table describes one small part of it:

"Actually, I felt like a prisoner trapped behind dark bars of horror. With my hair on end, my heart pounding, and scared stiff, I often cried out like a madman. I begged for mercy and clamored against the painful despondency that had taken hold of my spirit. But when the loud cries didn't fall on an implacable silence, they were answered by lamenting voices even more pitiful than my own. At other times, sinister laughter rent the prevailing silence. I thought that some unknown companion out there was a prisoner of insanity. Diabolical forms, ghastly faces, animal-like countenances appeared from time to time, increasing my panic."[29]

Doesn't seem like a great place does it? The Lower Zone is comprised of many areas. Not just a strange dark dimension that exists parallel to our own, but also right here, on the surface of the earth.

In the book, *Memoirs of a Suicide*, by Yvonne A. Pereira, the main protagonist of the book, Camilo Castelo Branco, who committed suicide when he was going blind because of syphilis, describes what it was like awaking in the graveyard where he was buried.

"Sobbing uncontrollably, I bent over the grave that held my wretched remains. Contorting myself in terrifying convulsions of pain and rage, wallowing in a crisis of diabolical fury, I understood that I had committed suicide, that I was in the grave, but that, nevertheless, I continued to live and suffer even more, so much more than before, superlatively, abysmally so much more than before my cowardly and thoughtless act!"[30]

Hence, Camilo, while his body, six feet underground, was deteriorating, felt he was alive, with all of the loneliness, pain and suffering it entails. Walking on the face of the earth, while incarnate visitors to familial graves passed through him, oblivious to his sufferings.

Camilo then left the cemetery, trying to ascertain what was this world that he had died into?

"I continued to roam around aimlessly, feeling my way along the streets, unacknowledged by friends and admirers, a poor blind man humiliated in the afterlife thanks to the dishonor of having committed suicide; a beggar in the spirit world, famished in the darkness; a tortured, wandering ghost without a home, without shelter in the immense and infinite world of spirits; exposed to deplorable dangers; hounded by malefic entities, criminals of the spirit world, who love to use hateful traps to capture individuals going through tormenting situations like mine in order to enslave then and increase the obsessing hordes that destroy earth's societies and ruin men and women, submitting them to the vilest temptations with their deadly influence."[31]

The Lower Zone is all around us, teeming with life, not of the benevolent kind. The type of life that we discarded as childish fears long ago. That our rational minds refused to consider, since we could neither touch nor see it. For even if there are multiple instances of unexplainable phenomena, unless we have positive proof, or see it on television or the internet, we are labeled fools to believe its existence.

Exists it does and it is there for a purpose. While we must go through trials in our physical life, in order to learn the valuable lessons assigned to us, once we end our studies; does everyone pass? No matter how pitiful our performance was? We aren't in a local kindergarten class where each participant gets a ribbon. God is love, and love can be tough love, the love that holds us to a high standard. A raised bar that ensures only those who meet the minimum criteria are allowed to enter the higher planes.

Thankfully, all who reside and wallow in criminality or mindless materialism with their sights set on earth are rescued in time. All spirits are given the period and assistance to slowly modify their behavior and attitudes to begin to look upwards and work themselves out of the pit and into their rightful place in a celestial city.

Howard's Escape

The errant spirits took Howard on what seemed like a long journey. The landscape grew increasingly dark, as Howard unknowingly descended further into the Lower Zone. Exasperated, Howard refused to travel on. The inferior spirits turned on him and beat him. The fight continued and then:

38

"We had a big fight and the fight turned into them annihilating me, which they did slowly and with much relish," he says. "Mostly they were biting and tearing at me. This went on for a long time. They did other things to humiliate and violate me which I don't talk about."

When Howard was no longer "amusing" to them, he collapsed on the ground, ripped apart, unable to move.

He lay there motionless for a few moments, completely spent. Then he was surprised by a small voice inside his head that said, 'Pray to God.'

He thought, 'I don't pray. I don't even believe in God.'

Then he heard the voice a second time, 'Pray to God.'

'But I wouldn't know how to pray even if I wanted to pray,' he thought. Whose voice was this, he wondered? It sounded like his voice, but the words were completely foreign to his own thinking.

Then he heard the voice a third time repeat the same message. His mind drifted back to his days in Sunday school as a child. "I tried to remember things I memorized when I was very young," he says. He struggled to think of something he could pray.

Then he managed to blurt out, "The Lord is my shepherd and I shall not want…"

When the people around him heard his attempt to pray, they became enraged. "There is no God and nobody can hear you," they cried, along with other obscenities. "If you keep praying we will really hurt you."

But Howard noticed something curious. The more he prayed and began to mention God, the more they backed away from him.

Emboldened, he began to shout out bits and pieces of the

Lord's Prayer, "The Battle Hymn of the Republic," and "God Bless America." Finally, he was screaming any fragments of God's truth he could muster from the moldy recesses of his memory bank.

It seemed to work! Even in the darkness, he could tell they had fled, but not too far away."[32]

There are two reasons why the gang retreated. First, Howard demonstrated that he was not similar to the errant spirits who first came to take him away. As Howard prayed, he would begin to appear brighter. His spirit would transform to a less dense state.

Secondly, and most importantly, the unfortunate spirits backed off because of the presence of high spirits. Howard and the inferior spirits couldn't perceive them at first. Higher spirits are more energy and less matter. Hence they are invisible, not only to us, the living on earth, but to even other spirits who are not as advanced.

To make themselves apparent, higher spirits must use their thoughts to make their form denser, only then could they be seen. For as Howard heard the voice in his mind telling him to pray, it proves a higher spirit was with him throughout the journey, waiting for him to exercise his free will and decide to reconnect with God.

Once, the presence of a heavenly spirit appeared, the others would retreat, well accustomed to the power of light. The malformed gang watched what would happen next from afar.

Howard's Review of his Life

On the other hand, Howard still did not notice the presence of his spirit mentor. He then started the more familiar phase of a NDE:

"As he lay there, Howard began to review his life. "I came to the conclusion I led a crummy life and I had gone down the sewer pipe of the universe. I had gone into the septic tank with other human garbage. I was being processed by the garbage people into garbage like them."

"Whatever life was supposed to be about, I missed it," he thought. "What I received was what I deserved and the people who attacked me were people like me. They were my kindred spirits. Now I will be stuck with them forever." Feelings of self-loathing and hopelessness filled his mind."[33]

The spirit mentor put a thought in Howard to begin thinking about his life. This is a commonplace occurrence in Spiritist literature. Those who have died are led to recall the major events of their life.

The review of our past life and our own critical judgment of our motives and actions are what sends us up or down. Not some tribunal of holier than thou hypocrites. Which is the fear of most of us who at one time or another disdained religion.

With good reason we have look aghast at the televangelist who preaches the word of God, while asking for more money for his personal use. No wonder multitudes want no association with the likes of such transparent duplicity.

But, this is the great secret, the summit of where you will end up. You are your own most severe judge. Yes, you who have rationalized away many wrongs and committed small transgressions because of cultural pressure. The list could go on and on, and I have done them all. We determine exactly the extent of our sentence.

The kind spirits around us are consistently more forgiving of our wrongs than we are. Why? Because they have perform such circus acts of circumvention themselves. Been there, done that, is their sorrowful thought as they see us as we look back on our life's story.

Next, Howard cried out to be saved by Jesus.

Howard's Ascent

That final gasp, the shout that laid bare his wish to not travel his current path, but to change direction and follow the higher, and many times rougher road, enabled Howard to see the spirit that had been with him the entire time.

"Howard was amazed at what happened next;

Within an instant, a brilliant light appeared that came closer and closer. He found himself bathed in a beautiful light, and for the first time he could clearly see his own body's miserable condition, ghastly for his own eyes to behold. "I was almost all gore."

Immediately he recognized Jesus, the King of Kings, the Rescuer, the Deliverer. "His arms reached down and touched me and everything healed up and came back together," he recalls. "He filled me with a love I never knew existed."

Then he picked up Howard, like one football player picking up a fallen teammate on the field, put his arms around him, and Howard cried like a baby in His arms. 'He carried me out of there and we headed to where God lives.'"[34]

Howard reported that next, Jesus had angels to help him access his remotest thoughts to fully review his entire life.

Howard looked back and saw his transformation from a young child to an arrogant teenager. An unloving and selfish person whose character was reinforced by his success at becoming a full tenured professor at the age of twenty-seven. Howard saw the extent of his failings by watching the reaction of Jesus:

"As they watched together, Howard could see the pain and disappointment on the face of Jesus. 'When I did these things it was like sticking a knife into his heart.'"[35]

We retain all, and by all, even the tiniest details, of our entire life while on earth. Hence, these records are used, for and against us, when we pass over. Our spirit retains each and every moment of our life, every scene in 3D.

The reviews can be painful, others have reported the same hurt and disappointment in watching the arc of their lives. For example, Gail, who had a NDE at the age of fourteen, describes her experience, as she remembers it in May, 2014.

"I was aware that I could communicate without speaking and that I could know all that I wanted to know. There was a feeling of peace and calm, unlike anything I've experienced since. Then came a judgment of sorts, where I was judged on the things I had done and the things I would do in my future life. This upset me as I felt it was mean to punish or judge me for things I hadn't done yet. I wasn't judged on big things, more small instances of intent. It was the little things that mattered and not the big things. Then I was told that I had to go back, which didn't make me happy at all as I knew that being alive would hurt."[36]

The Return

Howard was ready to remain in heaven, but he was told he would return. He woke up and was notified the surgeon was available and he was going into the operating room.

After recovery, Howard's life changed:

"When his strength returned, Howard began to devour the Bible. "Since none of my atheist friends believed me, I started memorizing verses and I would give them Bible lectures, but that didn't go over very well," he recalls.

He grew "desperate" for fellowship in a church, and began to attend Christ Church in Fort Thomas, Kentucky, part of United Church of Christ. Howard's pastor worked with him patiently, and after three years, Howard was ordained as a lay minister in his church."[37]

Howard's life took on a new meaning, he now understands the need to balance his spiritual and material existence. He went on to write a book about his experiences, as a lesson and a warning for those who deny any possibility of an afterlife.

Our time on earth is one of trials. Howard went through his events and came out a better person. Every one of us has an assigned lesson plan. Before we are born, we may even take part in determining the hurdles we shall cross. Obstacles that serve to guide us to learning more about ourselves and our innermost attitudes and morals to live by.

I believe that Howard was given a mission before he was born, to bring a light to others so they could find the right path. Howard's NDE was the catalyst, probably pre-planned to set him on a trajectory to write his books and bring his experiences and point of view to the world.

Chapter 5 – What is the Doctrine of Spiritism

This chapter is an introduction to Spiritism. What you should know about the beginnings and the doctrine of Spiritism before you decide to become a Spiritist or begin to learn about the spirit realm and how we live within its boundaries.

In essence, your soul will live forever. You will experience life after life in a quest to perfect yourself. You have a mission, the most important mission possible; to improve, to love, to be charitable. To be part of a grand plan to not only raise yourself, but your neighbors and the entire human race.

While in the spirit world we are bathed in love, each of us must learn how to love. Hence, for every wrong you commit, you will have to pay for it in this life or the next. And, the trials you are experiencing now are the results of errors you have committed in the past, plus a splattering of coursework that you have been assigned. Our suffering is for the noble cause of teaching us to love unconditionally.

How do we know all of this?

Jesus promised us more Information

"If you love me, keep my commands. And I will ask the Father, and he will give you another Consoler to help you and be with you forever…the Spirit of Truth. The world cannot accept him, because it neither sees him nor knows him. But you know him, for he lives with you and will be in you." New Testament John 14: 15-17

"But the Consoler, the Holy Spirit, whom the Father will send in my name, will teach you all things and will remind you of everything I have said to you." New Testament John 14: 26

What did the Consoler actually do? What did he contribute?

Spiritism states that Allan Kardec was the Codifier, who presented the Spirit of Truth (Consoler) to the world in the five books that Allan Kardec assembled. Kardec's books revealed the extent of the Spirit world, who is God and Jesus, why we are here on earth, how we should live and the doctrine to follow. That is all. The answers to questions that every one of us have spent nights pondering.

What is Spiritism?

The basic tenets of Spiritism are:

1. Love God.

2. Do unto others as you would have others do unto you.

3. Practice justice.

4. Forgive all who offend you.

5. Make amends for our own wrong doing.

The spirits revealed to us the basic facts of our existence:

1. Your soul is immortal.

2. You travel through multiple lives as a process to learn to love, be fraternal, and be selfless.

3. The goal of God is for every spirit to one day be pure.

4. There is no eternal hell, it is a station for souls who are materialistic and have an excessive love of self.

5. There are many levels of heaven. Heaven is not a place where we have eternal leisure, but one of on-going work to help others.

6. Life on earth is like a school. You are assigned events in your life and how you react and behave will determine your spiritual progress.

In the 1930's in Brazil, the medium Chico Xavier began

psychographing (the process of a medium writing under the direction of a spirit) messages and books sent by spirits. From the very beginning he was told to always follow the doctrines of Allan Kardec. Chico wrote more than 400 books by the time of his death in 2002. Within these books, the Spirits revealed information about Allan Kardec and the Spirit world's plan for our future;

1. When Jesus referred to the "Great Consoler", he was foretelling the arrival of the Spirit of Truth, which was codified by Allan Kardec.

2. For the earth to progress, the human race needs to understand that every action they do here on earth will have consequences in their next life.

3. The Bible was written by men under the influence of their beliefs and culture at their time. While the central spiritual message of love is eternal, the stories of the Bible, such as the Earth being made in six days are allegories and not meant to be taken literally.

4. We are being told this now because the human race is culturally and technically advanced to be able to accept these messages.

5. Spiritism is not meant to replace religions, but to supplement them with the knowledge of the basic doctrine of reincarnation and its purpose.

6. The spreading and acceptance of Spiritism will enable the world to begin a new age, where war is a thing of the past.

7. The Spirit world has planned these events and is guiding the earth through subtle interventions.

8. At some time in the future, science will definitely prove the existence of a soul and an afterlife.

As one can see, the tenets of our spiritual path and reincarnation have also been delivered to us via an alternative channel. That of the spirit world communicating directly to mediums to alert us of a life beyond our single human existence.

Spiritism and how it explains your trials on earth and a survey of what is the spirit realm like is all in my book, *Explore Your Destiny – Since Your Life's Path is (mostly) Predetermined*.

If you wish to learn more about how reincarnation works and why we must have multiple lives, please read my book, *The Case for Reincarnation – Your Path to Perfection*.

While all around us people who have psychic abilities or those who had NDEs experiences are reporting the same philosophy of love and redemption through trials.

I also chronicle how trials in my life, seemingly inconsequential and major events have shown me the power of Spiritism and what are the *7 Tenets of Spiritism – How They Impact Your Life*, in my book.

Chapter 6- Other Death Experience – Nicola and the son of her friend

This is a most unusual story of a friend of a woman who was pregnant, had a baby boy and the recollections of the boy just before his birth. The child, years later remembers where he was as his mother was in labor and the specific events the friend experienced as she went to help the boy's mother at the hospital.

This account is located on the NDERF.org site, which has thousands of NDE's from all over the world.

The actions in this story are a testament to the Doctrine of Spiritism. For without the knowledge presented to us by Allan Kardec about the organization and processes of the spirit realm, this story would be unexplainable. By reading and understanding *The Spirits Book*, which tells us we are immortal souls traveling through multiple lives in a journey of improvement to become pure spirits, we are able to greet the events in this story with a comprehension based on the love given to us by our spirit mentors and the Supreme Intelligence; God.

I will let Nicola introduce her story:

"My friend and I met as school teachers at the same school, several years ago. She was pregnant when we met, and she chose me to be present at the birth of her child, because she was a single mother and afraid of being alone. It was a tremendous honor to be invited into the delivery room because, even though I have children of my own, it was a fascinating opportunity to see a birth without experiencing the pain myself!

My friend delivered a baby boy named Michael, and it was an incredible experience. I joked to her that I saw her son before she did! (I saw his head poking out before he was born and she didn't have a mirror to see for herself!)"[38]

A perfectly normal occurrence when a friend has a baby.

Nothing out of the ordinary. Unfortunately, Nicola's friend died a few months after the birth of her son. The boy was cared for by his grandparents. The grandparents, on the son's mother side, lived in the same town and within the school boundaries where Nicola teaches.

Nicola and her friend were both school teachers, working at the same school. Nicola was pleased to see her old friend's son, Michael, in her class. Although, she never spoke of her friendship with his deceased mother, for fear it may show favoritism over the rest of the class. Nicola also didn't have a relationship with Michael's grandparents and they weren't at the hospital during Michael's birth.

The Extraordinary Occurrence

Michael was in Nicola's class when he was nine and a half years old. For a poetry assignment, Nicola asked her class to write about their earliest memories. As Nicola states, most of the children would write about kindergarten or of a favorite childhood toy, when they were toddlers. Then Michael raised his hand:

"Michael put up his hand and said that he remembers watching everyone from up in the sky, and being in his mother's belly before he was born. He said that when he was waiting to be born, he was invisible and he was in my GREY car with me on the way to the hospital while I listened to the song "Winter Spring Summer or Fall." (This is what he called the song. He likely doesn't know the real name, and he probably hasn't heard it since ... but it was "You've Got a Friend" by James Taylor. I used to have the cassette tape in that car!!!). This is bizarre because I did drive a grey car at that time and I haven't had once for the past 7 years (2 years after he was born). I can't imagine he even knows that song from today's radio music. My heart started to beat like crazy. How the heck would he know that? Even his grandparents wouldn't know that and his mom wouldn't have known that before she died. Even if somehow she did, he was only three months old when she passed. How would she tell him? I certainly never told her what song was on in my car on the way to the hospital so I can't explain this!"[39]

We have heard numerous stories of people with NDE's who clinically died at the hospital, left their bodies and watched events unfold around their corpse. Recollections of nurses frantically setting up equipment, reactions of friends in the waiting room and other specific details which are unexplainable, except by the famous saying of the fictional detective Sherlock Homes, "when you have eliminated the impossible, whatever remains, *however improbable*, must be the truth."[40]

The *improbable* being the existence of another world, another dimension from whence we came and shall return. Including, our ability to separate our immortal spirit from our physical manifestation and still retain our senses. For isn't this the greatest obstacle to overcome in our belief in the afterlife. One could easily believe that an orb of energy could escape our carcass and fly away to be reabsorbed in the Universal Intelligence. For this would still retain some sense of otherness, a mystery that many of us don't really want to discover. A deeply desired hope that when we die, all of our actions on earth are also left there. No guilt, no blame, no sense of failure, only love and forgiveness.

To have the realization before us, that indeed we are the same, with or without a dense body is either a wondrous discovery or a horrible moment of truth, depending on your point of view. Remaining who we are entails bringing with us to the other side our complete unadulterated set of memoires. Each good, bad or indifferent deed is stored, for us to contemplate upon for all eternity.

There are a series of books, all psychographed by Francisco (Chico) C. Xavier, and inspired by the spirit Andre Luiz. He was a wealthy doctor in Rio de Janeiro who died sometime around the end of the 19th century or the beginning of the 20th century. He chronicled his death, his time spent wandering in limbo and his rescue by good spirits to the celestial city of Nosso Lar. Which means "Our Home" in Portuguese. Nosso Lar, the name of his first book, relates his recovery and realization of his place in the universe. He discovers that heaven isn't a place for idleness, but one of self-sacrificing work on behalf of other spirits. Spirits who are on earth in physical form and spirits lost on various levels of atonement.

In subsequent books, Andre is a member of a team of spirits who travel to earth to assist us in our needs. Andre learns that we are compelled to be reborn to acquire valuable lessons, so we may pay for our wrongs in past lives. In the book, Workers *of the Life Eternal*, Andre goes further to detail the penalty of incorrect actions, "We will be compelled to regenerative work both during incarnation and discarnation, both in our corporeal existence and in the death of our body, both in the present and in the future. No one will successfully reach the peak of life eternal without first having learned the balance to do so."[41] He observed, after personally seeing the end of life experiences of multiple people, the passion to hold onto material objects, the regrets of wrong doing, the terrible physical inflictions caused by alcoholism or drugs, the totality of the effect on the spirit as it withdraws from the body. While, on the other hand, spirits who led a life relatively free from such actions, achieved a calmer death, a faster withdrawal from their bodies. The spirits who did not resist temptation experienced a much harder effort to let go. Even after full withdraw of their spirits from their physical bodies, these types of people were confused and required care to fully recover their thought processes.

Andre Luiz isn't the only one to present the salient facts about reincarnation to us, from Hinduism, Krishna in *The Garuda Purana* tells us, "Everyone creates their own fate. Even life in the womb is affected by the karma from a previous life."[42]

Buddha notifies us that our actions have reactions when he speaks about rebirth; "From a sound, an echo returns. A body creates a shadow. So, too, will misery come to him who does evil works."[43] The message has been consistent from the earliest times. The spirit world has delivered the certified letter, and it doesn't matter if we sign the return receipt or not. The process of payment and redemption is known to any who care to discover it.

Hence, the specter of not only living with our past but paying for our past is a realization that many of us would rather postpone, if not rationalize completely away. Because, which of us hasn't been regretful of past deeds. I know I have and I have plenty to pay for in my next life. Not a comforting thought before you go to bed.

But what is comforting, is that you are loved, warts and all. For every spirit knows they have been in the same shoes. All have been woefully inadequate during one life or another. Have comfort in the knowledge that the prize is worth the effort. Life in a heavenly city in the spirit world is indeed joyous.

Therefore, not only are we aware when we are parting from this world, but we are fully cognizant when we enter. Michael had the gift to remember his entry. For like all of us, Michael too, is an immortal spirit.

Michael continued his remembrances:

"Michael said that he remembers me stopping for gas and asking the attendant for directions to the hospital (TRUE). He said that he wanted me for his mommy because he liked my voice when I was speaking to the attendant. (I did stop for gas and I was kind of lost going to a rural hospital, so I asked for directions). Then he said that he remembers that the parking lot was partially closed for construction, so I had to park on a corner and run to the hospital. By this point my jaw was almost on the floor and the whole class was starting at me. I had never even told the class (or Michael) that I was at his birth. The class must have thought this was one crazy story."[44]

Michael's spirit was free from his new body as his mother was going into labor. For some reason his spirit rested, waiting for his birth, with his mother's best friend.

Proof of a Life Plan

Next, Michael told Nicola, what he saw and wanted, even before he officially entered the world:

"Then Michael said the most incredible thing - He said that while his "real mom" was in labor, he asked God if I could be his mom because he knew that his "real mom" wouldn't survive very long, and he was afraid of being alone on Earth. Apparently he was told that he couldn't have me for his "real mom" but that everything would be OK and he would still get to be around me during his life."[45]

Imagine the thoughts racing through Nicola's mind. Irrefutable facts are disclosed on the day Nicola traveled to the hospital in the identified car, the stop at the gas station, with the exact music playing, then Michael relays that he knew, he knew! That his mother was going to die in the near future.

Unless there is a plan for each of us, already set before we are born, how could Michael be certain that he would be motherless soon? The answer is there is a plan. A blueprint for each one of us. Our life is designed before we begin and we are part of that effort.

As our life progresses the spirit realm watches over us and responds to heart-felt prayers and pleas. Michael was worried about his life without a mother, but his fears were answered that all would be fine. He was even given the detail that he would be around his mother's friend in later life. How little do we realize that the path of our life is less free-will and choices made than we could consider possible.

Next Michael describes in exact detail what occurred when Nicola was in the hospital:

"Michael said that he kept begging for me to be his mother. He watched me go down the hallway from the birthing suite to the waiting lounge to make a phone call from a pay phone (true -- there was no cell signal in the hospital), and that while I was there I was very cold so I put on a sweater that someone else left on the waiting room chairs. By this point the hairs on the back of my neck were standing up. I hate to admit this, but I did find a nice warm cardigan in that waiting room and I put it on because I was so cold. I've never done anything like that before, but it was a small hospital and there were literally no

54

other people in the labor ward and I waited to see if anyone would come to claim the sweater, and no one did. I was so cold! I put it on and ended up wearing it home (Shame on me, I know, I still feel guilty about that. I've felt so guilty that I never wore it again, especially because it reminds me of my friend who ended up passing away. Regardless, I have to mention it because I've never told anyone about taking someone else's sweater, and it's a huge part of this story!!!!

Michael concluded by saying that he watched me make the phone call and put on the other person's sweater, and that's the last thing he remembers. He was born about thirty minutes after I went to the lounge and made that phone call."[46]

Nicola was completely alone in the hospital's labor waiting room, no one was there to see her take the sweater to use for a moment of comfort.

Nicola talks to Michael alone afterwards:

"Later, I privately said to Michael, "Yes, I was at your birth. How did you know all of that stuff?" His grandparents weren't at the birth and there was literally no way he would have known any of that. How could he make it up? He said that it's easy, he just had to think back to his earliest memories. He asked me why I don't remember being born, too and he said "It's OK, my life did turn out OK so don't worry about not being my mom".

WOW."[47]

Michael was given the gift of accessing his first physical memories. The spirit world must have thought that Michael required the comfort to reach back and realize he is loved by the invisible universe around him and that people on earth would be present to assist in his growth and coming trials.

Nicola then closes her account by attempting to make sense of the entire episode:

"I write this in all sincerity as my evidence that there must be some kind of heaven up there, if he could have memories of watching his birth and waiting to be born. I considered the idea that his mom speaks to him from the afterlife, and maybe she told him herself but how would she even know this information?"[48]

Yes, Nicola, you are correct, there is a heaven up there. Heaven is why we are here. To achieve the required spirituality, the necessary amount of love, charity, and fraternity, the constant adherence to justice and honesty we travel through multiple lives. God is not unjust, we are allowed infinite chances to become the pure spirits that we are destined to be.

Michael's mother could be watching the progress of her son and soothing his fears when he sleeps. For when we are at rest our spirits communicate with other spirits, providing us with moral reinforcement so we may strive on in our quest.

The spirit world doesn't just drop us on the planet and let us fend for ourselves. We arrive with a detailed set of goals, the environment set up for our success and a legion of spirit workers who track and help guide us onto the path of victory. All we have to do is listen.

Chapter 7 – NDE - Anna Discovers her Mission

After Anna's child was born, her doctor was called back to discover major hemorrhaging which was imperiling Anna's life. Anna was transported to a pool of light. Where her deceased family members were waiting for her.

This is a Spiritist interpretation of what she went through and what she saw. I don't judge her observations or feelings, just provide the reasons for her experiences. What lies behind her journey into near death? What kind of universe, organization, and processes orchestrate the sum total of those moments of other worldliness?

These are the questions we shall review. Anna A's NDE experience is gathered from the wonderful website, NDERF.org.

The Ascent into the Light

Anna seemingly had a normal childbirth. She was able to see her newborn son. The doctor had left after a long and grueling labor. There was no sign of excessive bleeding. Soon after the doctor left to clean-up, she started to go into shock from loss of blood. Anna describes what happened next:

"I heard them calling her and asking her to return. I had squeezed my eyes to the point of utter pain from the "freezing" that had overtaken every single limb, which I was sensing in such detail during those minutes. All of a sudden, I could only think of God and felt an urge to go, to let go and slightly opening my eyes, last thing I whispered to the nurse while grabbing her medallion of a cross hanging from her neck onto my chest, "Do you believe in God?"... She was engaged in saving me, but that second, she turned to me, removed the necklace and placed it inside my hand. And that's when I started floating."[49]

With her body failing, her spirit began to disengage from her dense matter. The question may be asked, exactly what separates from the body. Modern science considers the brain to be our total repository of all of our thoughts, memories and personality. While research is beginning to cite examples of brain-dead people remembering events that occurred in the operating room and other locations, there is no accepted scientific explanation for this phenomena.

Spiritism supplies the answer. Not only the answer but the entire cause and effect. We are not just a collection of cells directed by brain mass located in our heads. Yes, that is part of it, but what we feel, see, and touch about ourselves is just our physical manifestation. For our bodies are in essence a discardable spacesuit. Our souls, our spirit is immortal. It is Anna's spirit that ascended, leaving her body behind.

There is one more puzzle piece to complete the picture. Our perispirit, that which connects our spirit to our body. The perispirit is the channel through which the spirit absorbs all of the memories, actions and even attitudes that we experience while on earth. Every data point is recorded. Our innermost thoughts are saved and nothing is able to erase them.

Hence, when Anna floated, she didn't notice a long silvery cord that still connected her to her body. Like an umbilical cord, which feeds the baby, the connection from her body to her spirit still functioned. She still had the means to return.

Anna's New Body

After leaving her body, she climbs into the light. She discovers what she really is:

"The life I'd been living on planet Earth was an insignificant second of an experiment, which I'd volunteered for. The ME, the I wasn't Anna the lady who'd just given birth, but it was a light being - "LIGHT" in every sense. i was made of the same light as the one the pool was filled with. It sensed everything, felt everything beautiful as there can ever be, thought and understood everything and was floating around inside the pool

58

happily, FINALLY back HOME!!"[50]

"An insignificant second of an experiment", this is the timespan of your life on earth in relation to your total existence thus far. You now have a window into what it feels like to be immortal. Someday, the sun will burn out, and your memories of the earth, now a dead planet, will be distant.

As Anna realized, this is the manner in which you should consider your life. Whatever calamity befalls you, whatever situation you are locked into, is all but a moment of time, which shall pass very rapidly. Practice viewing your life from the mountaintop. Look down and see the obstacles are not as large as they seem. The worries not as great and the picture not as dark as first feared.

Next, Anna wrote, "which I'd volunteered for", in that sentence fragment the entire truth of our reason for being on earth is exposed. We reincarnate on earth. For many it's not an involuntary process, but one in which we are intimately involved. In the books inspired by the spirit Andre Luiz, psychographed by Francisco C. Xavier, he tells of people and couples in the spirit world who actively plan out, in minute detail, the arc of their lives.

They select their parents, who most probably, they have had in previous lives, their characteristics and the trials, the events they will live through. Happenings that will supply instructions they feel they require to improve.

Hence, the great milestones of your life are pre-destined. And you are the person who selected them. All design to enable you to reach your goal. The goal of improvement. The betterment of your spiritual knowledge, for one day you will become a pure spirit and not have to reincarnate again. Only if you wish to descend to a planet to assist others.

Anna also expressed the sensation of lightness. In the Spiritist books the words they use is less dense. Whereas, we on earth live in dense bodies and our senses only perceive about one eight of the world around us, in the spirit world, the real world, we are ethereal, we are less dense, and our atomic structure is different. We live in a different dimension than the one where physical earth resides.

Our form, our clothes are shaped by our thoughts. We are what we think we are. Spirits move by the power of thought. Spirits are able to walk, but they are also able to think where they wish to be and appear there at great speed. Anna examines her state of being more fully:

"And, "LIGHT" as in lightness, no gravity, no strings attached (that's how I sensed at the time), I was sooo happy that I wouldn't have to sleep, or eat anymore, no tiredness, no negativity, no anxieties whatsoever, and you float and float lightly, dancing and singing with no audiovisuals, you're just BEING, that's what you're for - TO BE!"[51]

Meeting her Family

As mentioned previously, when you reincarnate you are frequently with family members. For one of the laws of the spirit world is the Law of Affinity. Where like-minded souls are attracted together through shared values and interests.

Anna relates how she met her deceased mother-in-law and wished she could have played with her grandchildren. Then Anna found out:

"She "answered" - "Don't you worry at all! Before this child was born, we went together to all the gardens and lovely forests and we laughed and played and sang together. Besides, now that I'm here I can protect you much much stronger than if I were there, weak and ill"[52]

In this reply are two very important concepts about the spirit world, where we all come from. First, we are part of our own plan for reincarnation and our spirits merge into a physical body, beginning in the mother's womb.

Our spirits are connected to our bodies, when we sleep we are able to temporarily leave our slumbering cocoons and visit other spirits. Hence, Anna, and her baby in her womb visited her mother-in-law in the spirit world.

Secondly, when Anna's mother-in-law said she could protect Anna and her children better from the spirit world, it demonstrates the amount of interaction spirits have with us. Our spirit guides and family members watch out for us. Like hovering parents over their elementary school children. The children are too absorbed to notice, but their parents are present, ready to jump in at the first sign of trouble.

Anna didn't just encounter one relative, but many, and friends from the spirit world. All were happy to see her. They took her to a "library" and explained why she was on earth.

Anna's Job

"Apparently, I had a "job" up there and had left it "briefly" when coming to Earth because I'd needed to experience certain things and learn certain things in order to be able to continue my work"[53]

Now comes the shocker, life after death is like life before death. You still work. You are still productive. You are still learning, every minute, every day. However, the conditions we toil in aren't similar to our experience. We work in a location of intellectual stimulation, pursuing our passion, comfortable in the knowledge that what we are doing is for the good of all, not just to add one more trophy automobile to the boss's garage. Anna describes her feelings:

"Time and space had no phisicality, no validity. I'd call the whole thing as FREEDOM, the PERFECT FREEDOM, which every person I know aspires to, fights for, dreams of etc"[54]

But, in order to gain more productive positions in the spirit world you need to gather more experience. Just like in our world. The desire for increased responsibilities entails the need for training and knowledge. Therefore, Anna came to earth, with a mission. And not just Anna, for she was part of a team with a job

61

to do.

"However, these thoughts I'd filled into the manuscript I was in charge of had a great purpose, served a great purpose, which as a Light Being I knew, however, back into my human body, I don't have a clue, as if there was a veil administered upon my return. There were many other light being conducting similar work, and yet I knew that not every soul or light being is given such a task. Ours was a team destined to do this... Others were destined for other "work"..."[55]

It seems strange that a person who is given a task to accomplish is sent on a mission with no recollection of what that assignment entails. Although, you aren't just randomly set down on some beach and told to attack. The family you are born into, the events of your life are all methodically planned to guide you to your full range of responsibilities. Additionally, you have two items from the entire arc of your previous lives, your conscience and instincts. Your conscience has implanted all of the Natural Laws and your interpretation of the rules and regulations. Your instincts will alert you when to act and move forward or when to find other avenues.

Hence, you are set upon a relatively narrow road and as you travel you shall, without conscious knowledge, accomplish your jobs as you encounter them. You do have freewill to make the wrong decisions and to ignore all signs of your intended work.

Anna Learns About the Importance of her Work

Anna felt so comfortable, so at home in the spiritual realm, she wanted to remain. But then:

"Someone was telling me "Anna, need for you to go back"... That moment I felt earth-like sadness, which hurt piercingly what I'd been in that duration - that Light Being... And I found myself far from the pool and the library, but looking at the Planet earth from the space/cosmos, and a light being's had risen next to me pointing at the Planet, and a voice asking me "Look there (the planet)! What do you see?", I said "I see

Planet earth and I don't want to go back. This is my home, why are you sending me back there?". He soothingly calmed me (all sensory, no touches, no words), then asked again (oh, with such divine voice, an actual, physical voice), "Look again..... What do you see NOW?".. Suddenly I saw what the voice saw - "I see our planet and there are no borders dividing countries... The borders are gone!!"... He said "This is why you're going back. You have a mission."... And that's how I came back."[56]

Anna discovers that she is part of the mission to transform our planet. According to Spiritism, our earth is a planet of atonement. A place where we are reborn to pay for our past wrongs and to learn the hard lessons so that we may become better souls. Spirits who are full of love, charity, fraternity and honest in our daily dealings.

The earth is being guided by the spirit realm to become a planet of regeneration, where there are more good than bad spirits, where wars, envy and hate start to recede.

Conclusion

Anna, like all of us, are not just physical bodies with an organic conscious, that will one day fail and dissolve back into carbon-based compounds. We merely use our bodies as the key to enter another world. A world that serves as our college, in which we take classes, sometimes we enjoy the subject, others we hate and more often we are bored.

Even though, we may not adore all of our lessons, we must remember that we are being graded. Hence, if we maintain a good attitude and are able to continue radiating love to all, even during our difficult times, we shall emerge victorious from our adventure on Earth.

Chapter 8 - ADC – After Death Communication – David G.

David G. had an After Death Communication (ADC) experience which illustrates how the spirit world communicates with us and the power they have to speak directly to our minds. I take the reader through David's experiences and relate what the spirit world is actually doing.

David G. had an experience that changed his life. He started communicating with a deceased niece at her funeral. You can read his whole story at the NDERF.org website.

The Death of his Niece

On the day his niece died in a car accident, David felt strange, like someone wanted to talk with him. He felt guilt playing golf on that day, but he sensed his niece, Michelle, telling him it was alright. On the day of the funeral he described what happened:

"Two days later, the day of her Catholic wake, at the evening session, I had a sudden and undeniable verbal communication from Michelle. I was sitting with my wife in the second row at the funeral home before her casket. She said in the voice of a four year old, "Here comes trouble" and communicated without words that I should go out to the parking lot to meet with a young man who had just arrived. I could clearly see him distraught and teary-eyed with a small group of other young people her age in the parking lot though there was no window in the room. Over and over she wanted me to go out to him and I refused with my rational mind. There were no words at first other than "Here comes trouble" and "Go see him, Uncle Dave". I just knew I should go and I clearly saw the scene in my mind, the same way I was hearing her words. I sobbed heavily, overcome with a feeling of... awe? emotion? it's hard to say. I was just hearing her voice so clearly and seeing what was going on in a place I couldn't physically see. I just 'knew' what was happening, and where the boy was. I didn't know who he was, only that she said "Here comes trouble". I knew her boyfriend at the time, I had met him at the house. He was in the room in the funeral home with us. This was someone else. I didn't know who he was, I just knew he was there and that she wanted me to go to him.

After I delayed long enough (perhaps a few minutes?) there was no longer a need to go outside. The moment had passed and I felt it. I could see him leaving some of the friends, and moving with others toward the door of the funeral home and eventually into the long hallway crowded with mourners of all ages. It would be a while before he entered the room where I was with my wife and her family. As a part of me followed his slow walk toward the room, I continued the communication with my niece Michelle. She spoke so clearly, in a young voice I best remember.

I asked her where she was and why she was talking to me. She told me that she wasn't speaking to me directly, but that I alone had heard. She said it was a matter of openness to the experience. I asked her why her voice was that of a four year old. She said there was no actual voice, that she and I were sharing thoughts - thought energies? - and that my mind was putting a voice onto what was being communicated. She deliberately said in her young voice "I could sound like this", then in her 19 year old voice "Or like this", then in the voice of a 64 year old woman she would never be "Or like this". Each time my mind heard the voice clearly and knew what I was hearing. It was indeed my mind putting an audible voice on some other way of communicating. I just 'knew' it. It's so hard to put into words what I was experiencing. "[57]

This episode perfectly illustrates the communication between the spirit world and the physical world. Spiritism tells us that we all have the capacity to be mediums, to somehow communicate with discarnates (people who are no longer living on the physical plane). But, of course, some of us are better and more adept than others. David G. has that ability, since his niece told him that she was directing her thoughts to everyone in the funeral hall.

Spirits talk directly to us, by radiating their thoughts to our cerebral center, which controls senses, sight, hearing, touch and our psychic abilities. Thoughts are real in the Spiritual world, as in here on earth, they are the beginning of any actions, but more so in Michelle's new location. By finding a receptor, Michelle could by thought alone, talk to David in whatever voice she so desired.

There are two more details I would like to add. The first is that most certainly, Michelle was not alone in the funeral hall; there must have been other spirits there to help her control her thoughts and emotions after such a violent death. Secondly, Michelle must have been an advanced spirit, for most people when they die, go through a, at least, several day period where they are confused or even not aware they have perished. Therefore, for Michelle to have communicated so calmly and with clarity reveals her to be well acquainted with the spirit world and that upon her death, she realized she had accomplished her mission on earth.

Next David G. learns more from Michelle's side, the "other world", as the Druids called it:

"I asked again, or for the first time, where she was and I saw a blackness, a void, in which there was a spinning orb about ten feet tall to my perception. The spinning orb was the earth and it was spinning very fast - many revolutions per second. Two spiritual forms approached the spinning orb/earth. The spiritual forms I mention were to my perception some sort of misty beings - ghostlike - with some semblance of humanoid scale and size, and yet they were formless. They were human size only in reference to my point of reference, the reference in which the rapidly spinning earth was about ten feet in diameter. As one being said some sort of farewell to the other, the other lifted up in a large puff and disappeared as a funnel shaped mist onto the surface of the planet. In a matter of seconds it reappeared, this time as a small point of a funnel shaped mist lifting up and coming back to the same size and general shape it had before. It walked / drifted away with the first being as they discussed what had happened during that lifetime. I knew I had witnessed a human lifetime from another perspective, a spiritual form experiencing a single human lifetime and then coming back to review it with a friend/peer. It's hard to explain but it was so clear to me.

I also saw/felt/experienced total darkness that wasn't darkness, a void that wasn't a void but was everything and everywhere all at once. No time, no space. In that absence of anything I could be anywhere at any time just by thinking about it. All I had to do was to have a thought and I was there. Everywhere all at once. It was the most amazing, profound, deep experience I have ever had in this human lifetime. (Later that day and for days after this whole experience I journaled the whole thing extensively. I haven't re-read the journal but I have it in my possession to this day.)

I believe she also shared the moment of her death during that time we were speaking. She also communicated to me that I shouldn't share this experience with her immediate family as she came from a troubled family with a horribly abusive childhood. They wouldn't understand at this time, nor should that abusive energy be part of the equation at that time. I honored her wishes."[58]

David G. saw the spiritual world from Michelle's perspective and he saw her judgment after she died. For a moment he too existed in the other dimension, where time and space is altered, and all exists is a world of vibrations, where our minds control the energy around us. Energy to make us look that way we desire, energy to have us appear to be dressed as we wish.

Michelle must have chosen a mission to be part of a dysfunctional family, either to assist the family or to make up for past wrongs or a combination of both. Whatever the facts, even after she passed away she was still trying to protect her family.

David G. also let Michelle possess his body at a later time for Michelle could use David to convey to her how much Michelle loved her mother. David G. showed all of the effects of a medium allowing a spirit to use them to communicate to the physical world.

"I actually dropped down onto the floor in a fetal position weeping. My sister in law asked what was the matter. My wife knew. I lay there trying to get a grip and while I was there in that space between physical reality and soul awareness something happened again. Michelle came through. Not verbally, not in words, but lovingly. She asked if she could use my body. There's no way to say how these things happen. There's no real progression of events. It's just all there all at once. Like that void, that place of nothingness where everything is all the time. Just think about it and you're there. Any time any place. It's all one. We're all one."[59]

In Spiritism, David G. would have been trained as to what to expect and how to allow a spirit to temporarily control his body, all the while maintaining the ability to dislodge the spirit when he deemed it necessary. Also, to make sure the situation never spirals out of control, there would be other trained mediums in the room to come to the rescue if the possessed medium felt weak. Again, most probably, Michelle had other souls assisting her in using David G.'s body to convey her message of love.

David's New Calling

David G. proved himself most useful. Therefore, given his great talent to help others in need, he started upon a new career.

"I've developed a healing arts practice of my own that became a vocation. Since retiring from my career as a postmaster, and even in the years before retiring, I've turned that vocation into a small business. I practice as a vocation though, not as a business. It's not about money. The money comes all by itself when it's needed. I've never had to worry. Working with people, usually with spiritual and emotional blockages, had been my calling. PTSD (posttraumatic stress disorder) seems to be a common thread among my best clients."[60]

Notice how David G. said, "It's not about money", this is one of the most basic rules of Spiritism, you should not charge money for the gifts that God gives to you; you should freely give to others to help them in their time of need. Knowing this, the spirit world

68

provides for those that contribute their talents freely. David G. is not correct when he says, "The money comes all by itself when it's needed." There is a team of spirits directing events to ensure that his needs and the needs of his family are taken care of.

We are so much closer to the hand of God than any of us could ever believe. We grow up in a society where God is at best distant to most of us. Thankfully, I have found out, late in life, as David G. has, that God's love is so much closer than we realize.

Chapter 9 – NDE - William H Detects the Universal Intelligence

William H had an NDE in 2003 and he found himself surrounded by beings made of light, who could communicate by thought. What does this mean to us and how it should change your thinking is explained.

William H had a heart attack in 2003 and soon found himself out of his body and taken to another place. The link to his full story, can be found by looking up William H NDE on the NDERF.org website, which contains many interesting NDE stories.

He describes what occurred:

"My whole life, it turned out, had been practice for the moment of dying: my higher soul stepped forward, speaking reassuringly about how it had been through this so many times before. While my lower soul, this lifetime's personality, went mute in the face of the vast Unknown, my higher soul catapulted into It with one last sigh of joy and gratitude: What a glorious Creation!"[61]

Almost immediately William realizes that we all travel through multiple lives. Upon his near death experience he re-learns the truth, that we are all immortal souls, who are reborn on earth to study to be better. Although, he calls it "my higher soul", what actually occurred is his spirit detached from his physical body. His perispirit, which is connects his spirit to his body, is the form which allows communication between the cerebral center and the spirit. His spirit contains all of his memories of his previous lives. We are a combination of our spirit, perispirit and our body, we only temporarily inhabit our physical bodies and rely on our organic brain for the time we are here on earth.

The Over Soul

William then describes what he felt in his body made of

energy:

"I was fully awake when I realized I was myself a sphere of communion. A sphere of aware light. Surrounded by an infinite number of other spheres of aware light.

As I experienced it, then, the Sphere of Universal Communion is an infinite space of aware light that is occupied by all the individual spheres of aware light that ever have or ever will exist. As if it were One Mind, occupied by all the individual Ideas it ever has or ever will conceive. Or a timeless, limitless, Oversoul, occupied by all the individual souls that ever have or ever will enter the realm of time, space, and personality. As I said, I do not pretend to know what its true name is, but the relation between the Whole and its parts — and between parts and parts — this I can still see with diamond clarity."[62]

All of us have a unique signature that radiates from our minds. Our thoughts are constantly transmitting, like a radio tower, out to all around us, which travels to the end of the universe. Conversely, we receive wavelengths, which contains thoughts from intelligences that surround us. Hence, as William sees it, we do live in a "sphere of universal communion", in continuous communication and we live in that state thanks to the benevolence of God, the Oversoul, who created all and set the natural laws that we must follow.

Next William writes:

"Each of us, as an individual sphere of communion seems the embodiment of two complementary halves: Understanding and Memory. While Understanding seems the principal characteristic of the higher soul, Memory seems to be the principal characteristic of the lower soul. As I experienced it, Understanding is our individual portion of the limitless Knowledge of the One Soul, the evolving insight we possess into the Way of the One, our individual spark of immortality. Memory, on the other hand, is the accumulated impressions of all the lifetimes we recall, the sum of all the personalities we have yoked to our soul, our enduring storehouse of mortal

71

treasures."[63]

William is a just a bit off in his interpretation. Your perispirit, which is connected to your body, allows you to retain the memories you create while in your physical body. Yes, William is correct that it is your organic mind which first stores the memory, but all of them are uploaded into your spirit via the perispirit, where if you wish, you could recall in life like detail every second of your favorite recollections or every millisecond of your life. You may ask, why can't we recall memories from our past lives? Some young children do, when the ties between the perispirit and the brain is forming, but most grow out of it.

What we do retain, is our conscience and instinct. Therefore, listen to your conscience, it contains countless years of experience and attempts to direct us on the right path. Heed your instincts, again, our accumulation of lives should make us better aware of when our decisions are in question.

Lastly, when you do pass from your current life, your memories of past lives do not return immediately, rather, they come back slowly and you accustom yourself back to your "real" life as a spirit.

Feelings of Love

William also perceives the love of the beings around him:

"Other individual spheres of aware light, many of great depth of Understanding with the Memory of thousands of lifetimes, generously taught me lessons to bring back and make use of in this lifetime. Such, it seems, is the loving-kindness of our collective ancestors, who care so deeply that this era of transformation is one of metamorphosis and not one of atrophy."[64]

Love is what God wants us to radiate. This is why we must journey through lives filled with strife, to absorb the lessons required to allow us to love all in every circumstance. To feel what others have felt and to reach out to help whenever it is needed.

William doesn't yet realize that this is God's plan and that in our solar system, Jesus is our loving Governor. He is the one who directs the destiny of the earth.

William takes what he has felt and found that it carries over to our world:

"Although it is much more difficult to perceive here than in the Sphere of Universal Communion, we are no less individual spheres of communion here than we are there. Once I had experienced what it feels like to recognize myself as a sphere of aware light in the bodiless state, I found I had become sensitive enough to perceive myself as that same sphere of communion here with a body. And sensitive enough to recognize that everyone else is a similar sphere of aware light, as well."[65]

While we reside in our cumbersome bodies, our abilities to truly identify with others, to share thoughts, emotions, and love is diminished, we all should recognize that all humans are spirits, in many different levels of perfection. It is our duty to assist others in their quest to become better. Sometimes that means helping and other times it could mean some tough love, so they will be able to understand the lesson they need to internalize here on earth.

Chapter 10 - NDE - Sara Finds Out How we are Assisted by the Spirit World

Sara A is an interesting case. She hit her head, after overdosing on different types of medications and woke up a changed woman. She remembered, via lucid dreams what she experienced while she was unconscious, but she didn't have the usual all in NDE white light type of experience. Her story is on the NDERF.org website.

This case illustrates how our encounter can not only modify our attitude toward life, but also our entire physical body and alter how we process our sensory input and thoughts. Sarah begins by relating how she fell to the depths of despair.

> "I had officially hit rock bottom in my life. My prosperous career had ended abruptly due to an accident that caused a debilitating back injury and I was wallowing in the depths of fear and victimhood. The doctor told me that my back would require surgery if I ever wanted to have a normal life again but I had no means to pay for it. Angry bouts of pre-cancerous skin tumors had begun to pop up all over my body. I lived through my days lying in bed in and out of consciousness with the drapes drawn, with daytime reality TV playing in the background. I existed in a debilitating mental state with my emotions fluctuating between depression, anxiety sadness, anger and futility. Thoughts of ending it all began to enter into my mind. I over-medicated daily with a cocktail combination of pain meds, antidepressants, anti-anxiety pills, and alcohol in an attempt to try to numb out all the physical and emotional pain I was feeling."[66]

Here is one of the common themes of many NDEs, suffering. Why is this? Why must we suffer here on earth? Why must we suffer at all? Unfortunately, there is a good answer.

Being trapped in a material body affords us the opportunity to learn what is not possible to apprehend in the spirit world. While certainly, one can gather intellectual knowledge, the building of

74

our emotions, of faith, charity, honor and love are rooted in the pain and suffering we are exposed to in the physical world. The Spirits Book backs up this thesis, in the secondary question to question 175:

Would it not be happier to remain as a spirit?

"No, no! For we should remain stationary; and we want to advance towards God."[67]

Hence, there is no shortcut. No easy path for redemption. We can't lie our way out, we can't hire someone else to take the punishment and there is no one to bribe to let us off the hook. We must pay the bill with our own time and labor.

In the book, *Memoirs of a Suicide*, Camino Blanco, the spirit who inspired the book, visits the wards of a heavenly campus, where suicides are recovering, after a period of time in the Lower Zones. At the end of the long tour through the wards of the truly pitiful spirits, Camino is told that all will recover eventually. The method is described by those whose love and compassion will direct the care of the mournful spirits.

"Pain the Teacher will correct their anomalies and reconcile them with the Law! God is Infinite Mercy, my friends! He wants his people to live in harmony with the eternal beauty of his laws! And since we know that these laws are incorruptible, it is up to us to obey and respect them so that we don't wind up having to drink the bitter gall of the consequences that we created for ourselves with our freewill when we left the natural and luminous pathway."[68]

"Pain the Teacher" is exactly what Sara was experiencing. Her suffering focused her thoughts. Sara's mind was honed in on her life like a laser. She thought of ending her life because of what she had reviewed; her mental and physical life had totally deteriorated.

Sara had reached the end of her rope. Only then did she determine to try once more to ask God for help.

"I became so lost one day that I knew I had reached the brink to utter darkness. I cried out in agony from my heart asking for God to save me. I was mad at God during this time and blamed him for my predicament. Previous to my accident I had prayed for help in finding happiness in my life and had been in the accident instead. Things had become much worse instead of getting better. At the time of my first prayer I remember feeling guilty and ashamed because even though I had all the material comfort I needed and the perfect husband, I still didn't feel happy inside and that something was missing."[69]

This passage reveals so much about our life on earth and how we are led by the spirit world. Sara tells us that before her accident she had prayed for help in finding happiness. Even though she had the money to buy what she desired and a wonderful husband, she still felt lost inside.

God had given her enough luxuries that any third world person would have traded their left hand for. While, millions of people exist in a loveless marriage, Sara knew her husband was worthy of her and loved her. Yet, like many of us, she still felt a lacking, a hole in her being. Ask yourself, what could have God supplied to her that would have made any difference?

Winning the lottery would have supplied a few moments of exhilaration, then the same longing would have returned. Any material gain could only provide a temporary relief from her despair. The void that she felt is only fillable by her own mind. God knew this. Her spirit guide knew this. Hence, they really did answer her prayer. Events were set to enable her to realize the solution to her problem.

By the way, be careful for what you pray for, you might get it. As in the stories of Aladdin, where the genie grants the wishes in ways you did not consider, the spirit world may also deliver you what you need. Not what you want.

Sara's Accident

The very evening after she fervently prayed a second time for

God's help, she felt mentally refreshed. She and her husband went to a restaurant and as she approached she felt immense energy all about her. A large presence loomed that heightened her senses and caused her to look in every direction.

At the restaurant, she drank excessively. Her husband managed to get her to the car, she threw-up on the drive home, next attempted to walk to the house after they arrived. Whereupon she fell down and hit her head on the sidewalk. Her worried husband took her to the hospital.

Sara reports what happened at the hospital:

"That first night in the hospital, I could feel all the inner emotional pain of all the people, and even the doctors and nurses. I noticed that there was a very calm peacefulness that was radiating and generating love from my heart center and that it was having a soothing effect on everyone around me, calming them and healing away stuff they had taken on. Strangers at the hospital befriended me, and hospital staff went out of their way to converse with me, much to the curiosity of my husband. I knew why but felt the need to say nothing but just share a state of higher consciousness with everyone who came near."[70]

Sara started to feel the thoughts and feelings radiating from others. Her mind, which for Sara and all of us is a beacon of energy, sending thoughts and receiving them, became more in tune to the stream of feelings from others.

Andre Luiz, the spirit who spent time in the Lower Zone before ascending to the celestial city of Nosso Lar, wrote in his book, *In the Domains of Mediumship*, about the time when he was told how our minds are like the amount of energy transmitted to a light bulb and how it affects the amount of light displayed. Andre was interested in the analogy of our thoughts and the light bulb. He wished to know how the energy of the light bulb is related to our mental forces. His instructor quickly perceived his thoughts and explained the relationship:

"The bulb, in whose interior the light is produced, disperses the photons which are elements of nature that vibrate in physical movements particular to them. Our soul, in whose intimate ambient the radiating idea is processed, projects the condensed spiritual elements into various mental forces. The world acts one upon the other through the radiation they emit, and the souls influence one another via the mental agents they produce."[71]

Hence, our mind does send out energy, not photons, but another form, of which our science has not yet explained. The normal functioning of our body supplies the power, derived from our food intake, to allow our brains the electrical and chemical power for our neurons to trigger to internally form and emanate our thoughts. Andre takes this logic and extrapolates to its logical conclusion.

"Just as we on Earth have an understanding of the chemistry of dense matter by cataloguing its atomic units, we can also study the make-up of the mind. Cruel thoughts, rebellion, sadness, love, comprehension, hope and happiness have individual weights and make the soul more dense or subtle, In addition, we can define it magnetic qualities. Each mental wavelength possesses its specific coefficients of energy expressed in silent concentration, speech or written word."[72]

If this statement is true, then by analyzing the wavelengths radiating from our minds, we are able to ascertain the general thoughts of a person, this explains how spirits are able to mentally read our minds. Sara begins to display the same talent.

The Transformation

Sara felt her body completely morph into a sensing organism. She writes:

"I now felt completely conscious and awake in every cell of my body for the first time in my life and I was very aware that I was seeing the world through entirely new enlightening eyes. I knew everything was going to be okay in my life and I had no fear, only anticipation and an excited feeling to hurry up and get started with whatever was about to happen."[73]

The spirit world not only healed her body, but enable Sara to use her full potential. There is an example of the spirit realm assisting a woman in the book, *Missionaries of the Light*, where the spirit Andre Luiz watches another spirit, Anacleto, manage the healing process. Andre asks if he could see a demonstration of the benefits of the procedure, and Anacleto points to a woman and tells him:

"This morning she had a bad argument with her husband and entered a serious state of inner disharmony. The small cloud surrounding her vital organ represents fulminating mental matter. The permanence of such residues in her heart could cause a dangerous illness. Let's help her."[74]

Andre then saw that Anacleto, with the help of an incarnate Spiritist, directed the energy of the Vital Fluids, in the form of a ray of light, toward the woman's heart. Andre describes the healing that he witness:

"Besieged by these magnetic principles, the small amount of black matter enveloping the mitral valve slowly moved away, and as if attracted by Anacleto's strong will, it reached the upper tissues, scattering under the radiating hand along the epidermis. Then the spirit magnetizer began the more active phase of the passes, discarding the evil influence. He made a double pass over the epigastric area by lifting both hands and immediately bringing them down very slowly past the hips down to the knees, repeating the same pass and operation over the area several times. In just a few moments the infirm woman's body returned to normal."[75]

Andre was amazed at the speed and completeness of the healing. Next he was curious to know, what would have happened to the woman, if she didn't visit a Spiritist Center. Would she be able to heal herself? Andre is told anyone who is living a religion that follows the path of the good, will receive spiritual assistance, as long as they ask for help in prayer and trust in God.

Therefore, Sara's plea to God, wasn't just answered by the Divine Entity, but most probably a team of spirits sent by God. They had given Sara a new gift. A power to be used for the good of all. She describes her new ability:

"From that moment on I was able to feel the pure vibration of a person and all the fear and insecurity floating around them just like bad computer viruses that could easily be swept away. Something alive inside of me was able to speak to others energy and reassure them that everything was really okay and it was all just debris that was swirling around. I knew inside myself without a shadow of a doubt that everything was and always had been okay and would continue to be so always. I knew there was a plan. I was able to sense fear energy as dense and weak and crying loudly. This never went away and I help clients today sharing this gift, among others that I received."[76]

Along with her new ability, her head and body ceased hurting and she recovered her ability to move her torso without pain or stiffness. For the first time in years she was pain free and able to discard all of her medications.

As others reported in their NDEs, Sara talks of a plan. She doesn't know the details, but she knows there is one. Like other spirits, before she came to earth, she created a plan for her life, part atonement for past wrongs and part labor for the good of others.

In her plan, she divided her life into two sections. The first half of her life was one of a normal self-possessed person. She describes her intellectual growth:

"There was so much still to download and understand that what I came back with was so immense and it would take some quite a bit of linear time to accumulate in my body mind so I began to meditate to speed up the process. I suddenly felt the craving to do this and discovered that I was instantly really good at meditating, even though I had never done it before. Previously, my ability to focus even for a moment was impossible because my mind was a lot like a 5 year old on a sugar high. Before this experience I was extremely impatient and incapable of sitting still or listening or focusing for longer than a few seconds."[77]

Her description of a short attention span could fit almost all of us. Our culture does not promote introspection or contemplation of any sort. We are trained to move from one channel to the next, in search of any available stimuli, except our own thoughts. Now, given the ability to use her cranial capacity as she should, her learning accelerated, her intellectual boundaries have greatly expanded. Even into areas where she shied away from in the past.

"My new understanding of numbers, math, and physics was both interesting and ironic because all my life I had struggled with even the simplest arithmetic. I still don't possess the knowledge to solve math problems, but I know I don't need to. I just have to apply the energy itself now and not try to figure the math part out. But I love numbers and equations and everything science related just the same."[78]

The instant understanding of complex equations is indicative of how spirits communicate. By wavelengths, numbers, ratios, transforming thoughts into math equivalents, are aspects of communication between higher spirits. While lower spirits still converse in words, using languages known to us on earth, there is a universal idiom to those who roam the universe and live on higher planes. Sara's spirit knows this, although unable to completely connect with her spirit and full memories, she is acquainted with the practice.

The Result

The combination of the gifts bestowed and Sara's own dedication made her a new person. Ready for the second phase of her life. First she healed herself:

"I had battled with my angry pre-cancerous skin tumors during my mentally ill state of existence, which I now completely understood were simply a numerological equation of energy that resulted in matter that was out of alignment to the

81

harmonious balance of nature (no other way of describe it).   In human terms my cancer and back injury were the direct result of my mental and emotional state and were manifesting into physical dis-ease. I had no fear toward death or illness anymore so I simply started directing or harnessing or aiming mathematical equations of harmonious love toward my ailments without really trying but allowing, and it manifested a harmonious physical result. Everything that was out of alignment in my life, both emotionally and physically healed quickly and efficiently."[79]

There are examples of healing in Spiritist literature. In the book, *Missionaries of the Light*, Andre Luiz again supplies us with his view from the spirit realm, there is a section that deals with a young woman who is being obsessed by spirits who wish revenge on actions she had taken in a previous life. Alexandre, Andre's mentor, tells him why the young woman is able to successfully resist the barrage of bad thoughts that errant spirits are aiming in her direction:

"Only patients who have willingly made themselves their own physician achieve a positive healing; the principle is the same in the dolorous field of obsession. If victims capitulate unconditionally to their adversaries, they will surrender completely and become possessed after becoming an automaton at the mercy of the persecutor. If they have a weak and indecisive will, they will become accustomed to the persistent actions of their persecutor and will become accustomed to the circle of irregularities, a situation very difficult to correct, because little by little, it will become a pole of strong mental attraction to the persecutors themselves. In such cases our activities are nearly limited to simple tasks of assistance aimed at results far into the future. However, when we find patients who are interested in their healing, taking advantage of our resources in order to apply them to their spiritual evolution, then we can foresee immediate gains."[80]

Hence, as in Sara's case, you too, whether you have a physical or mental illness, if you emphasize your spiritual strength and willpower, reject bad thoughts and maintain your positive energy, you shall be actively assisted in your recovery by your friends in the spirit world.

Along with her increased mental powers and refreshed body, Sara has a new philosophy of life.

"I can sense now the most efficient way back to the love of source is to just trust in the flow of nature and to love ourselves and others selflessly. We have the ability in this lifetime to gain mastery over our human thoughts and to become conscious observers of our continuous states of being humans and so we can learn in a more efficient, and non-judgmental way. I know now that the beauty is in the journey and not the destination. The more I allow myself to sift through my life experiences, I'm able to truly see all sides of the coin and learn traits like compassion, patience, and selfless love. Then I can become spiritual and fluid again and move back into the more spiritual states of awareness and into the light."[81]

Sara intuitively found the Doctrine of Spiritism. That we are all immortal spirits, who reincarnate to improve our souls. Our need is to practice love, charity, fraternity and live honestly. Selflessness is the key. Help others, encourage all, be kind to everyone should be a daily ritual.

It is not surprising that Sara comes to the conclusion that she did, for Spiritism reveals that the Natural Laws of God are implanted in us. They are part of every spirit. We have the right to ignore them, but they are always there and our conscience provides detailed interpretations for each code, each regulation in the pantheon of laws.

Therefore, we don't need books like the ones I have written, we have no requirement for dogmas or rituals. The Bible is superfluous and all of the literature written by saints and others telling us how to behave and think aren't necessary. For we contain the complete code within us. We just don't listen.

This is why the Bible and other teachings are important. Not to expose a new set of divine laws, but to convince our minds, our emotions, our passions to reflect for a moment and listen to our conscience.

Our path to ascend spirituality is tattooed inside us. A mark we can never erase. The map to happiness and bliss is clearly defined. Each road sign is unambiguous. We only have to heed the directions supplied us. How many times have you read in the Bible, where Jesus said, "If anyone has ears to hear, let them hear." This is precisely what was meant. If you would just listen to what you are saying to yourself, you will know!

Sara is tapped into dimensions beyond our comprehension. She sees, senses and feels the energy that we walk in every day.

"Now as a practicing spiritual medium, I experience daily validation from clients that our souls really do live on eternally. I also know from the spirit world that this plane or dimension is just a tangible, shapeable, learning matrix that has no emotion, except for what we as humans attach to it (like the wave-particle thing). And there are other worlds besides this one. I can even see the energetic grid in the sky now; and I also see millions of tiny light beings or energies that look just like fireflies buzzing around everywhere. I'm able to see an energetic force field around all things."[82]

Again, Sara is speaking from the Spiritist playbook. The universe is full of life. Spirits transport themselves from place to place at the speed of thought, hence the fireflies buzzing around. Sara was blessed to see more of the world than we can.

I know of a person in Rio de Janeiro who can see spirits. He says they move in rapid motion, like robots, each movement precise. They are beings less dense than we are and composed of more energy. Their thoughts transmit into action.

The spirit world has revealed to us that we can only determine a silver of what is around us. In the book, *Workers of the Life Eternal*, dictated by Andre Luiz and psychographed by Francisco (Chico) C. Xavier, a spirit comments on the capabilities of incarnates:

"Notwithstanding the progress of scientific investigation, ordinary humans can currently perceive only about one eight of the plane where they spend their existence. Sight and hearing, the two doors that could expand their intellectual research, continue to be greatly restricted. For instance, let us consider sunlight, which compress the basic colors that can be seen by corporeal eyes. We are only able to see colors that go from red to violet, and most people see nothing past the last five, which are blue, green, yellow, orange and red - they fail to detect indigo and violet. However, there are other colors in the spectrum that correspond to vibrations that the human eye is incapable of detecting. There are infrared and ultraviolet rays, which the human researcher is able to identify imperfectly but is unable to see visibly."[83]

All that Sara has experienced, all that people who have had NDEs since humans populated our planet is real and explained by Spiritism. Why was Spiritism not sent to us earlier and the Doctrine only exposed in the 1850's? Because, the human race wasn't culturally and technically advanced enough to profit from the teachings until now.

Yes, we are traveling through a relentless materialistic stage at the moment. This shall pass when more souls seek to balance between their side that wants to accumulate goods and their side that comprehends the importance of their spirituality.

◆——— • ◆ • ◆ • ———◆

Chapter 11 – NDE - Amy - A Young Woman who May Have Attempted Suicide

Amy was married and a mother of a four year old at the time she experienced her NDE. She had chronic pain since she was seventeen, due to fibromyalgia. Amy had been taking low doses of the medicine prescribed to her and still had side effects. She knew, if she took more than what she had been using, the results would be unpredictable. Feeling that she had nothing to lose she followed her doctors exact prescription and took the full dose of medicine to lessen her pain. She quickly fell into a coma.

Amy's NDE was found on the NDERF.org website and her full account of her story is can be found by using the URL in the Bibliography section of this book, by the name of "Amy C".

The Cause of Amy's NDE

Amy had good reason to try to lessen her discomfit. Fibromyalgia is a very debilitating disease. According to Wikipedia, fibromyalgia is:

Fibromyalgia (FM or FMS) is characterized by chronic widespread pain and allodynia (a heightened and painful response to pressure). Fibromyalgia symptoms are not restricted to pain, leading to the use of the alternative term fibromyalgia syndrome for the condition. Other symptoms include debilitating fatigue, sleep disturbance, and joint stiffness. Some people also report difficulty with swallowing, bowel and bladder abnormalities, numbness and tingling, and cognitive dysfunction Fibromyalgia is frequently associated with psychiatric conditions such as depression and anxiety and stress-related disorders such as posttraumatic stress disorder. Not all people with fibromyalgia experience all associated symptoms.[84]

The day to day struggle for Amy must have been immense.

One can well understand the despair and the search for an ultimate solution to her difficult trial. Amy describes the fast effects of the medicine she swallowed:

> "I went to bed after taking all three and within minutes felt myself begin to go numb. Then the inside of my nasal passages swelled up and I couldn't breathe at all. I couldn't even open my mouth I was struggling to get air, but could not. My entire body felt like it was mummified. I couldn't call out for help, and it only took a couple of minutes before, the struggle was over."[85]

She felt, as others before her, an urge to rise and a sense of leaving it all behind, even her pain.

In the Room

Next, and this is where her story diverges from any others I have read, she enters a portal where others are also present. Sensing other souls who have been released from their bodies isn't the difference; what happens next is:

> "The next thing I remember is pulling through some kind of a portal along with many others. It felt like I was in a waiting room. There were many others coming through and I began to watch them move in. I watched a group of about three teenage boys come through who had an energy and way about them that was very obnoxious. They were big and seemed stupid and even a little threatening. As I was looking at them, it came to me that they had died in a car accident where they had all been drunk. Another woman came through who looked to be in her fifties or so. She was quite the chatterbox and was talking on and on. I listened to her for a minute and she told me how proud she was of her "sexy body" and how well she had taken care of herself in her life. How "good" she'd "looked." She proceeded to try and show me her body. I noticed that she had a fake color of skin, like she'd either been going to tanning booths or laying out under the sun for way too long. Her hair looked to be a fake color of blonde and even her breasts looked like she'd had implants, which I seemed to just

87

know without having to ask. It came to me that she'd died of skin cancer. She seemed to want to talk about herself a lot and I became bored and moved on. A lot of others came through. This room or area did not feel very bright to me, and despite the fact that I was receiving somehow, information that these people were dead, I hadn't accepted that, because everything felt so real and natural. So seemingly, alive. Nothing felt shocking or strange. I was simply very curious about what it was all about."[86]

The people in the room were all dead. Yet, they acted the same as they behaved in life. This is the realization that may be the most difficult for people. We are not turned into loving angelic beings as our spirits leave our bodies. Unfortunately, we are what we are in life and death. If a deceptive conniving unscrupulous person suddenly dies, they are the same after passing over. As is the pious gentle soul who cared for many.

Yet, slowly after we pass over to the real world, those who realize the love and caring surrounding us and the part we must play in our path to perfection, our mental facilities increase. We begin to regain memories of our past lives. We see our life and world from a new perspective.

Amy saw a hint of this when she reported later in her account:

"I've lost my temper in horrible ways and I have had great trouble with forgiveness, and yet, I felt only Love and understanding through the entire life review. What it felt like to me was that I was being given the opportunity and Gift of being able to stand back and more fully understand and love myself. I was able to feel exactly what others around me had felt during my life. I understood how everything I did and said and even thought had touched others around me in one way or another. I was able to even enter the minds and emotional centers of many who had been around me, and understand where they were coming from in their own thinking, how their own personal views and lives' experiences had brought them to the places each stood. I felt their own struggling and their own

88

fears... their own desperate need for love and approval, and more than anything, I could feel how child-like everyone was. With every person I viewed, including myself, I was able to See and Feel with a Higher Mind and Eye. And the feeling I had toward everyone was nothing less than what a loving mother would feel for her own children at toddler age."[87]

I believe how Amy discovers her feeling for all of us on earth is how the higher level spirits who determine our path and guide us appreciate the human race. Chico Xavier told the world, that we have no idea how much love God and Jesus has for all. This should be no mystery, after all why else would Jesus send his messengers to earth to proclaim, time after time, how we should behave and believe. The latest herald being Allan Kardec, who not only codified the Doctrine of Spiritism, but revealed the entire spirit world to us. How we arrived here on this planet, why we must reincarnate, and what is life like in the spirit world.

Next Amy met another woman in the room.

"There was a young woman who came up to me. She had beautiful, almost greenish eyes, and the most lovely shade of red hair. She began to tell me about herself. She told me that she had died with the feeling that was similar to drowning.. slowly blacking out with no way to breathe. And yet, I wasn't sure if she actually had drowned. While she told me of her death telepathically, I actually experienced at a certain level, what she felt. I was able to physically parallel her own memory. She started to give me orders, "Tell them this.... etc." "Tell them that, etc.." She was giving me personal information about herself. I had no idea why. But I politely listened. One thing she said was that she wanted me to "Tell them that I loved to sing." She gave a quick/impromptu singing performance for those immediately around us, and I thought her voice was beautiful. I was also awed by how she was free during her performance to actually elevate herself and move through the space around her without touching the ground. It was like watching an underwater dance without the water. I don't know why I wasn't more shocked, or why I accepted this so well. I also noticed how at a certain part of her song, her beautiful red hair seemed to grow LONGER! I thought it was interesting that she could choose to have longer hair at will. This young woman (maybe close to age 19 or 20) also told me how she had regretted not "hanging in there." How it "would have been better to stay" and work out her issues. But she also told me to "Tell them how free I feel now." [88]

Remember the red head woman who sang, she comes in again later in the story. And in your mind, put this thought, coincidences aren't necessarily by chance, many are manufactured by the spirit world. For us here, in our cocoon, safe in our little world, what appears to be random events often are not.

Another interesting facet is Amy's observation of the young woman's hair growing longer. In the spirit realm, our minds shape our bodies. Our thoughts make us appear as we believe we should look. Hence, the woman was changing into her true "self".

In the books, psychographed by Francisco (Chico) C. Xavier, there are numerous instances of spirits changing shape and features to correspond to their mind's eye of themselves. In one book, by a different medium, a spirit presents himself to another group of spirits as his appearance in one life, then changes into another person from his life before.

The power of our mind is greater than you think. This is why we are shackled to this planet until we reach the required maturity to handle this immense gift. After all, do you let your fourteen year old drive? No, they must wait until they have been trained, demonstrate responsibility and pass a test.

We are here on this earth, because we haven't yet verified our capacity to handle the great responsibility of our potential strength. No one in their right minds would let an immature child drive a vehicle which could harm others and correspondingly God doesn't let us off this closed campus until we behave correctly.

Next, Amy notice how people started to find each other and

form cliques, just like the closed groups in High School.

> "I remember that we had congregated into a much bigger and brighter room or area where there were many, many others present. Everyone was so busy talking and getting to know each other. It felt similar to the scene in a High School cafeteria. People even seemed to want to quickly find others they related to or felt at ease with, and there were even little "groups" that began to form."[89]

What is different about the after death experience, and this again is a revelation, is not that we are separated into two groups. Most religions throughout history have preached the good rises and the bad descend. But that we are separated into many groups, we land where we are attuned to others like us. The spiritual and compassionate rise up to souls like themselves, the deceitful gather together. Murders and hardened criminals are herded to another area, where they can enjoy each other's company until one by one a decision is made to change their behavior and beliefs.

Next, Amy discovers what each in the room had in common.

> "At a certain interval, I noticed a man move into the room. I sensed something about him. He felt safe and balanced to me. I just knew that I could trust him to tell me what was going on. It STILL had not occurred to me that I might be dead. And I wasn't sure I'd accepted the fact that these people were deceased, either. So, I moved toward this man (and another note. moving didn't really involve walking, just intent of desire to GO) and approached him with the question, "Who are you?" He looked at me and I realized he was a kind of teacher or Guide for this group. He explained that he had died in a truck accident. He had been a truck driver by profession. He was a Latino man. He told me that he was not a perfect man, but that he had Mastered Humility. I know that sounds ironic, but when I was with him, I could feel truly, that he hadn't a shred of self-regard or as we'd say, "pride," about him. He explained, that he had come to help teach them importance of humility to this group of people, because they had been so self-absorbed in

their lives, they hadn't been able to learn vital lessons and had aborted their own lives. He seemed to be telling me that in one way or another, these people had "Committed Suicide." [90]

The young boys who died in a drunken car crash, the woman who died of skin cancer as a result of too many trips to the tanning booths, these aren't considered suicides in our culture. They are deemed to be unlucky or made bad choices or a host of other excuses that ignore our personal responsibility to maintain our bodies.

When we reincarnate, we are given a form to use for the full term of our plan. For the same reason students are expected to take care of their books until the class is finished, we are tasked with the same obligation.

Not only had the group neglected their assigned physical bodies, but they chose to skip class. Instead of learning to be free of the material world, to engage in love and charity for their fellow humans, they turned inward and concentrated their energies solely upon themselves. Missing an opportunity to take that next step in personal responsibility toward becoming a pure spirit. A spirit who loves unconditionally and knows that to serve is the greatest calling of all.

In the spirit realm, the type of behavior that cuts short your life is called "unconscious suicide". You didn't take an open and deliberate step to end your life, but a series of decisions, that you knew, deep inside you, may lead you to an untimely end. You rationalized each phase as being inconsequential and wanted the pleasure to much to measure the possible long term risk. We see this type of behavior every day, on the streets and in the TV shows which bombard us with false choices, between one mistake and another. The only choice is how much of our hard earned money should we sacrifice for a momentary inclination.

Their curriculum was abandoned early. These poor souls will learn that the penalty is to stay on earth, in a not so pleasant location, until their normal time would have been up. Then, they will be assisted by spiritual workers who will lead them to spiritual

92

centers where they shall acquire their responsibilities and prepare themselves for their next reincarnation. Hopefully, the lesson will be so ingrained, so in their next life, they won't even think of escaping their duty again.

Amy understood this to be the case when she discovered:

"He explained how he needed to teach this group of people how vital it is to let go of themselves. How to lose their obsession with themselves. How they will be stagnant in all progress if they cannot unchain themselves from their own self-obsessions. He had to teach them the importance of humility. And yet, he shook his head, smiling slightly, and he implied that there was still very little he could help them with, without their bodies. His hope was to instill more of a passion for what he had to teach, strong enough that it would leave a seed of Light that might stay with them through their sojourns."[91]

The "Seed of Light", will be all they possess when they wander in the Lower Zones, neither in one of the celestial cities or the dark abyss, for their allotted period of time. When the spiritual guides come to gather members of the group, they will think back on the advice given to them when they first passed from their life.

The process of reincarnation will help this group of people. Slowly over the course of centuries, they shall grow in wisdom and caring. Each one destined, someday, to become a pure spirit.

Reincarnation is the vehicle to transform each of us. Each blemish and imperfection is removed as we travel through varied life events. Every trial demonstrates what we should or shouldn't do in our next existence.

The concept of reincarnation is present in many religions. This should be of no surprise since the messages all originated from the spirit realm. Here are three examples, from Christianity, Hinduism and Buddhism, of what we have been told regarding the need to be careful in what deeds we commit, for in the next life we shall have to atone for our wrongs.

"Jesus: Be merciful that you may obtain mercy. Forgive, so that you may be forgiven. As you judge, so you will be judged. As you serve, so will service be done to you. And whatever you measure out, that is what will be returned to you. [The Gospel According to Matthew]

Krishna: Everyone creates their own fate. Even life in the womb is affected by the karma from a previous life. [The Garuda Purana]

Buddha: From a sound, an echo returns. A body creates a shadow. So, too, will misery come to him who does evil works. [Three Sermons]"[92]

Amy Leaves the Room

In her conversation with the guide, she finally realizes that she too is dead. She asks the guide:

"I asked him point blank, "If these people are dead, what am I?!" I don't know why it took me so long to grasp the fact of this reality. He explained gently, "They are dead. You are in between. You are as if in a coma. You are not the same." [93]

At this point she realizes she must leave. She walks through the room toward an exit and has an unpleasant experience.

"As I moved toward the corner of the room to leave, at least a couple of the drunken, stupid boys suddenly lunged at me with words like, "She's alive, touch her!!" It was very creepy. They were actually grabbing at me and trying to yank me back toward them. They even tried to make sexual advances. I was horrified.

So, I now believe that some of the dead if not all, still have many earthly or worldly desires.

Looking back at that part of my experience, I was astounded by how earthy, how even animal-like people can be on the Other Side. One might expect that upon entering through Death's Door, there would be sudden enlightenment; that maybe

94

everyone would realize absolute goodness and choose Light and a fresh start, possibly becoming more angelic and purified, but in that place, everyone came in exactly as they'd been before."[94]

As stated earlier, there is no magical transformation upon death. Louts are still the same. People who are rude and disrespectful do not change. This is why we must suffer through our time on earth. For only by experiencing that which we should not do, can we internalize the lesson so that in our next life, we don't commit the error again.

Amy started to wander into new territory:

"When I left that initial place, I began to move quickly, and I felt that I was safe and comfortable. I felt enveloped in Love. There was someone tending to me, and I seemed to be at absolute peace with this person. There was so much light coming from this person's face, I could scarcely see any features in detail, but faintly remember slightly wavy, dark hair. And I believe this Guide was male. But even so, I felt a very maternal sense toward him. It was as if he were like a mother to me. So, I hesitate to label him with a gender. I'm not too concerned with that matter, though. I will refer to this Guide as male though, to make things easier for writing purposes. If I knew his name while with him, then it was taken from me upon return to my body because I no longer remember it. (I wouldn't be shocked to discover that much memory was pulled from me in regard to personal details of my Guide, because even my faint memories have been proved painful for me and have made me ache to return. I can't imagine remembering more. It would make being here so much harder.)"[95]

Amy felt what others have, immersed in an ocean of love. A feeling which is almost impossible to describe to we here on earth. Our lives are bombarded with a multitude of emotions during our waking hours. Socrates told us of the difficultly to learn and to know the truth while alive.

"While we have our body, and as long as our soul is immersed in this corruption, we will never possess the object of our desire: the truth. In fact the body brings forth in us a thousand obstacles due to our need to care for it. Moreover, it fills us with desire, appetites, fears, a thousand chimeras and a thousand follies, so that, while in it, it is impossible to be wise, even for an instant. However, since it is not possible to know anything purely while the soul is united with the body, one of two things will happen: either we will never know the truth, or we will only come to know it after death. Freed from the insanity of the body, we then will converse – hopefully – with individuals likewise freed, and we will know for ourselves the essence of things. That is why true philosophers prepare themselves to die, and why death is no way seems fearsome to them."[96]

"Freed from the insanity of the body", is the core truth of what Socrates is telling us. Our ability to concentrate, to give ourselves to love, think fraternally are all restricted due to our encapsulation in our body. Of course, this is the plan all along, we are in our physical forms precisely to be affected by waves of emotions. Only by surviving being suffocated by the rushing waters of materialism, jealousy, envy, selfishness and other negative thoughts can we begin to comprehend how to resist these temptations.

Amy also finds out another truth; we aren't allowed to retain perfect memories of our time in the spirit world. Why? Because, our memories would be so strong as to make us long to return to the spirit realm as quickly as possible.

In the book, *Between Heaven and Earth*, dictated to Francisco C. Xavier, by the spirit Andre Luiz, a woman, named Antonina, is given a chance to meet her deceased child (Marcos) in the Spirit world. She finds the child is happy with his life in heaven. She feels wonderful about the experience. When her spirit is put back into her body, the team leader (Clarencio), with whom Andre and Hilario are assisting, tells them:

"Our friend cannot hold on to the memory of what occurred," stated Clarencio.

"Why not?" asked Hilario.

"Very few spirits are capable of living on earth with the visions of life eternal. They need the environment of inner twilight. A full memory of what occurred would result in a fatal longing."

But the Minister patiently explained: "Each stage in life is characterized by special purposes. Honey may be tasty nectar for the child, but it mustn't be given indiscriminately - too much and it becomes a laxative. While we are in the earthly envelope, we cannot stay in contact with the spirit realm too long or our soul will lose interest in struggling worthily till the end of the body. Antonina will recall our trip but only vaguely, like someone who brings a beautiful but blurry picture to the living arena of her soul. But she will remember her son more vividly, enough for her to feel reassured and convinced that Marcos is waiting for her in the Greater Life. Such certainty will be sweet nourishment for her heart."[97]

The message we are hearing is that contact with the spirit realm is too enjoyable, a feeling of peacefulness and love that we would constantly long for, if we remembered its existence. One of the recurring themes of NDEs is the person who is in contact with the spirits, tell them that they wish to stay and not return to their life on earth, but are in the end told, "You must go back. It is not your time yet."

Amy Learns About the Universe

Next, Amy was given the great gift to be able to sense the universe as a spirit does:

"We were traveling upward, I suppose. My own vibration was changing. There was a big change in frequency. Like I was tuning into a different radio station on a grand scale. I was out in the Universe, and I was being given a kind of show. Like having an astronomy teacher speak on the beauty of the

97

Universe while lying under the stars at night. But I was out there amidst them. And this part seems to have been made foggy for me since my return, but I remember vaguely that during this scene, I saw something like holographic words and numbers move in front of me past the stars... and it felt like I was being downloaded with information. I felt at that time that I understood EVERYTHING. That I felt the full truth of Laws and Order in the Universe. One thing that I held onto was the beautiful MATH of the Universe. I remember coming to understand that there was a supreme and perfect kind of MATH that was in and of ALL things that existed. I remember being told something about Einstein! I was so excited. It was such a pleasant experience. I was also shown how there is a kind of clock-work in the sky. How the stars themselves actually hold a sort of map or mathematical Key to everything that is! "You are written in the stars," I was told! EVERYTHING is! I recall how THRILLING this part of my NDE was for me."[98]

Amy didn't realize it, but she was shedding her dense spirit, which had been trapped on earth with her, and transforming it into a lighter and higher spirit. A spirit who had the ability to immediately know the universe, to comprehend the completeness of God's design.

When Amy said she felt like information was being download, what was actually occurring is that she had access to information that had always been in her spirit. She discovered that she already had the set of Divine Laws inside her. We all do. We only need to follow the good advice of our conscience and learn not to rationalize away reasons to perform good deeds.

Amy Learns About the True Extent of Our Lives

With all of the new found information, Amy is able to finally grasp why we are here:

"I'd been taught in my life that we had ONE life to live (I'd never even considered reincarnation), and that some people get to have the most incredible luxury and wonders that anyone

98

could imagine, and others are "tested" because of their "valiant spirits" and have to deal with terrible miseries to "prove their strength", while still others.. like small children all over the world, are born to suffer through starvation and disease, rape, mutilation, even years and years of torture, only to die and then "get their just reward." This didn't seem like much of a "test" to me. It just seemed insane. I couldn't make logic of it. When I begged religious leaders for answers, I was told that "sometimes God let's wicked people torture good people so that He can punish the wicked for their deeds... otherwise, He couldn't punish them for anything." The whole system just seemed sick to me. I couldn't completely respect this notion.

In my NDE though, I came to understand that most of us have lived much, MUCH longer than we could even fathom. That our lives that feel so very long are infinitesimal when placed in the Whole picture... which for that matter, cannot even be framed. I was shown how every single individual through their own free will chooses paths that MATHEMATICALLY take them to the circumstances of their next existence or life. That NOTHING at all sits in accident or chaos. That every single aspect of our lives are ruled by NATURAL Laws that we placed ourSELVES in! That in a sense, we create our own worlds. I was shown how one can never assume either, that if someone lives a life of suffering that this is because of "evil" deeds. Many may CHOOSE a life of suffering because of what it Awakens in them or to help another, etc. We can NEVER EVER assume that we can be accurate in guessing why each Being lives the life they live. I cannot describe the relief... the refreshing, peaceful balm this Knowledge was for me. To finally gather this Truth that I'd yearned for all of my life... That all IS Good! That there IS sense and beauty all around. That no one is just "free-falling" as it had seemed before! That God doesn't just get to toy with us as He pleases with random ideas of tests, including rewards and punishments that just depend upon His current mood or mindset. While in this experience, out in the vast expanse of stars and planets, moons, and Knowledge, I Knew complete Trust for what felt like the first time. This was bliss for me. I had lived in fear and distrust and panic for 30 consecutive years."[99]

Amy just put the kernel of the Doctrine of Spiritism into two paragraphs. We travel through multiple lives, each life is a series of planned events. Like an undergraduate list of classes required to graduate. You, the student, is shuttled from class to class, where hopefully, you pick up something valuable from the lecture. And if you don't, well, then you retake the class.

What you think are your life changing decisions are set up for you. Coincidences didn't led you to your present situation. The spirit world in partnership with you, laid out a blueprint. Random encounters, weren't random. The people who you were raised with, brothers and sisters, aunts and uncles, parents weren't by chance.

In one sense this is a bit frightening, the foreknowledge that our life on earth will contain suffering at times. On the other hand, it is extremely exciting. You are being trained. Your destiny is to be a higher spirit. To live forever in the bliss described by Amy.

Amy Learns About Herself

Next Amy is blessed with the opportunity to review her life. A practice so few of us perform with complete honestly and self-awareness.

"My Guide stood by at a certain time (It is very difficult for me to place any of this in chronological order, as time felt so different there. It was almost as if many things happened at once, and yet separately. So there are parts of this experience, I can't honestly place in any order) and he lovingly stayed as my support while I had a kind of life review. I never felt chastised at all, even though I know I've been very cruel at times and have hurt many people. I've lost my temper in horrible ways and I have had great trouble with forgiveness, and yet, I felt only Love and understanding through the entire life review. What it felt like to me was that I was being given the opportunity and Gift of being able to stand back and more fully understand and love myself. I was able to feel exactly what others around me had felt during my life. I understood how everything I did and said and even thought had touched others around me in one way or another. I was able to even enter the minds and emotional centers of many who had been around me, and understand where they were coming from in their own thinking, how their own personal views and lives' experiences had brought them to the places each stood. I felt their own struggling and their own fears... their own desperate need for love and approval, and more than anything, I could feel how child-like everyone was. With every person I viewed, including myself, I was able to See and Feel with a Higher Mind and Eye. And the feeling I had toward everyone was nothing less than what a loving mother would feel for her own children at toddler age.

It was actually comical at moments. I could feel how the "Elders" as I will call them (these are those who are Helpers on the Other Side, who have Mastered themselves in many or all ways, and help work with us.) see us and find so much humor in the way we do things. It might seem brutally annoying to consider when we are in the midst of a great argument or drama that is playing out in our lives, that the Elders view these things very much like when a mother sees her two year old scream and cry and bop another child on the head with a stuffed animal. The mother doesn't want her child to "fall apart" and become hysterical and cry. She feels for her child, but at the same time, she sees a little bit of comedy in how seriously the child takes what is usually a trivial drama. She continues to love her child and thinks the world of it, hoping it will go on enjoying the day, living and learning."[100]

Amy presents us with two vital facts about ourselves and the spirit world. First, she illustrates how we should love and look at ourselves from the point of view of the other person. Love entails forgiveness and understanding.

Like any of us, at times we feel wronged and we blame the transgressor. We attribute a litany of ill will against the person who is the target of our scorn. We fail to sit back and place ourselves in

101

the shoes of others. Yes, sometimes, there may be a true desire to inflict harm and even for this we must forgive. Since that desire usually comes from some tragedy in the person's past. We should understand the difficult trial they are in and pray for their eventual success.

But for most of the time, the transgression is an innocent oversight. We should realize how all of us are constantly distracted by the vicissitudes of life and often lack the resolve to fully examine our actions upon others.

Secondly, Amy echoes the sentiments of the spirit world that I have read in other Spiritist books. We are looked upon as children. Barely able to decipher between right and wrong. When we reincarnate the hopes are high, but the expectations are low.

Unfortunately, the vast majority of us fail to fully utilize the opportunities presented to us. We waste the effort on surviving the trial by feeling sorry for ourselves and turning inwards, instead of using the opportunity to help others more, since we required assistance and we now realize what people really need. A helping hand, a kind gesture or a shoulder to cry on.

Whatever occurs, positive thoughts are continually sent our way. Cheering us on and gently guiding our movements toward the next lesson.

Amy Returns

With her new found knowledge, Amy felt comfortable and at home. It was a sharp jolt when she was told it was time to return. She shook and resisted the idea of leaving what was so wonderful. A place of respite, away from the confines of a dense body.

The spirit world showed Amy the future for her loved ones without her. Again this is a recurring theme in NDE's, not only is our future determined, but when one variable is altered, the new path of everyone we could have come in contact with is calculated.

"He came closer to me and I was comforted and he calmly

102

encouraged me to be strong. He told me to look to my left. As I did, I saw a school bus pull up in the distance. A small child was escorted out and brought to me. I recognized that it was my own daughter, who at the time was only four years old. She had been asked in her sleep to come in spirit to help me. She walked up to me, tugged at me a little and sweetly said in an encouraging voice, "But Mommy? Who will take care of us?"

Love on the Other Side, at least in my experience is so much bigger, so much more full than here. And you are more honest with your Love. You cannot turn others away who are in need. At least that was my experience. And there was no way I could have turned down my own daughter's plea. Without hesitation, I answered, "Oh honey. I will, of course." My daughter was then escorted back to the bus.

My Guide smiled knowingly and reminded me that he was not forcing me to go back. I looked at him and back at the planet Earth, feeling so frightened, still not wanting to depart and separate from him. The pain of division still seared through me. I cried and told him that I wasn't sure I could do it.

He said, "Look to your right." I looked to my right and saw a holographic figure. It was my own mother. It was a view of her in the future, and she seemed tired and in need of help. I will not go into detail here, because I want to respect her privacy, but I felt myself lean toward this futuristic hologram with the desire to touch or help it somehow, even though it wasn't presently occurring. It felt alive to me, and I noted that it seemed as I leaned toward her that I was a Gardener, wanting to prune some foliage.

The hologram faded out and my Guide said, "You see? It is time. You want to go."[101]

The other revelation that Amy tells in her account, is our ability to detach our spirits from our body when we sleep and talk to other spirits. Amy's daughter was escorted from her sleeping body and allowed to meet her mother in the spirit world.

103

Amy understood that one of her most vital missions on earth is to raise her daughter. Parenthood is a sacred duty, for we are preparing other souls for their destinies. Fortifying them with good intentions so they may improve themselves in their life.

Amy returned to her body. Her guide asked her to point herself toward earth and return. She came back, her spirit, connected via her perispirit for her whole journey, joined once again to her body.

Feeling her entire body fill with electrical energy, she fully regain the ability to breathe and feel. Her husband woke up and saw her adjusting to life once again, asked if she needed an ambulance. She replied that she would be fine.

Amy tells us the results of her sojourn in the spirit realm.

"Since that time, everything has changed for me. My health has returned. I get stronger and stronger each year. To my own surprise, I found the day after this event that I felt well, except that I could not eat any meat at all. Nor did I have any desire to. I've been a vegetarian since then. I eat a lot of raw organic foods. I don't eat anything with chemical ingredients, and keep my food very pure. My children and husband eat mostly this way too now, and we are all feeling great.

I could no longer continue with the religion I grew up in. This was not easy for me to walk away from, but I couldn't stay and maintain my own personal Truth and integrity. And yet, I have gratitude for having grown up in that religion and trust that it served its purpose for me. I am also at peace with the religious choices and needs of others.

I found I desired much less. Within the first week after my NDE, I was cleaning out my house, wanting to get rid of many things, a lot of decor, music CDs that I didn't find in harmony with the vibration I desired, etc. I lost my desire to want to shop as much as I had, previously." [102]

Amy, who felt pain every day due to her condition found a new lease on life. Her mental condition, her love and compassion, has influenced her body and allowed it to heal. While, many illnesses are naturally occurring, we can always maintain our positive attitude, pray and meditate to strengthen our resolve and heal ourselves.

Amy let go of her overwhelming material desires. Knowing that all matter is transitory. Only our spiritual self is eternal. Our knowledge, love and compassion stay with us, all other baggage is discarded.

Whereas, we use shopping to fill a void, find temporary enjoyment, for whatever exact purpose, the root cause is the same; we place our inner peace in a connection to the earth. Tethering ourselves to the planet is counterproductive. We should concentrate our energies on freeing up all ties, all restraints that aren't useful in our everyday lives.

One More Coincidence

The spirit world is wise. They realized that Amy could have awakened from her near death experience thinking this could have all been a dream. Even if she believed, others may have broken her resolve by questioning her visit to the other side.

The other shoe to her NDE dropped on her soon after she recovered.

"Within a couple of days, coming back from my NDE, I stumbled upon a woman who was being consoled by many others. When everyone had dispersed, I asked her what was the matter, and she told me that she'd just found out that her daughter had died. She'd been found in Southern California and she didn't know why or how she'd died. I asked to see a picture of her daughter, having the strong intuitive sense that I'd met her daughter on the Other Side.

The next day, she met me at my house. She had a black and white picture of her daughter, but I recognized her, right away. I said, "Did she have a pretty reddish color to her hair, and the most unusual green eyes?" She answered, "Yes, she did." I told her about my NDE and how I'd had this beautiful girl come and speak to me and ask me to give information to her family. I told her all that I could remember her daughter telling me, and it all made perfect sense to the mother. She told me that shortly before the death, she'd heard from others (she and her daughter had been estranged) that her daughter had begun to sing and had loved it, passionately. There was private information I was able to offer that gave this woman much comfort. I told her of her daughter's regrets in not having learned more while here. We learned a week later or so, through the coroner, how she'd died, which confirmed for me, what the young woman on the Other Side had said to me about her death and what it was like." [103]

Amy's experience is one more point of light for the rest of us. The spirit world, fully conscious of the immense power of the internet, is betting on the proliferation of real stories by real people from all corners of the world.

It is popular in our culture today to question the existence of God. After all, there is no concrete proof. Well, there is evidence all around us. Like children who can't find what they are looking for when it is starting them right in the face, millions of us are doing the same.

The spirit world isn't going to give us the answers to the test. It is our responsibility to discover the truth. The truth is laying about all over, we just have to open our minds and our hearts to see it.

Chapter 12 - Bronwen's Two NDE's and the Plan for her Life

Bronwen experienced two distinct near death experiences (NDE), separated by approximately three months. The first was the result of a head injury and the second was a spontaneous occurrence at a New Year's Eve party. Her feeling of joy and love during those episodes was remarkable.

Bronwen's story is posted on the NDERF.org web site. The link to her complete posting can be found in the Bibliography section.

Her First Experience

While Bronwen was using a tree as a handle for climbing, a branch gave away and plunged her, headfirst, onto a sandstone rock. A fall of several meters. Next she felt:

> "I found myself traveling rapidly upwards into the sky. I had an immensely joyous feeling of lightness. I remember looking back at my crumpled body on the rock below and observing that "I" was not my body. I could see everything below me very clearly. Below was the Hawkesbury river, and the beautiful bush surrounding it. I was heading towards some very beautiful cumulus shaped clouds. I had no fear, only joy."[104]

Rising upwards, Bronwen looked back and saw the love of her life looking at her still body. Feeling a rush of emotion for her boyfriend, she returned.

Like others, an overwhelming bath of love and joy enveloped her. Words do not do justice to the warm light and soothing radiation which permeates our whole being.

Once a person experiences that sensation, they know nothing can compare to it. This is why the spirit world allows only a peak at the enormity of what awaits us when we return.

Many people ask, why can't we retain our past memories? Part of the answer lies in the difference between the two worlds. Time and time again, we hear accounts of people who didn't wish to return to our brutal planet. Where we exist to learn, pay our debts, and assist others. No, unanimously, everyone wished to stay, only the reminder of their loved ones and unfulfilled tasks on earth caused them to return.

Imagine the constant longing and sorrow at being separated from perfection. Worse than any effect of being spurned from your ideal mate. The person who you thought would have been the love of your life. That pain took months to years to dissipate. The loss of swimming in a bath of love would be a thousand times worse. With our regret at losing that which we so long for, our effectiveness on earth would be greatly diminished.

Her Second Experience

The spirit world wasn't finished with Bronwen. My feeling is that they wished to speak more with Bronwen during her flight up from the earth, but her desire to return was too strong. Hence, the spirit realm manufactured a second rendezvous.

Bronwen describes the circumstances:

"My (same) boyfriend and I were visiting a friends New Year's Eve party. The party was in the main room of a small house, and was packed with people. It was before midnight. I remember feeling vaguely discontent, as if I wasn't where I really wanted to be. I was standing about one meter from the only door into the room, looking across the room at my boyfriend. Suddenly I was no longer in this room, but facing an enormously tall angel. Surrounding both of us was radiant light."[105]

Out of nowhere, with no physical act that could be responsible for her encounter, Bronwen was transported to a different dimension. The spirit realm wished to meet with her one more time.

"I knew this angel, and he knew me. I felt no fear, only joy and immense happiness. We communicated non verbally. The angel was 'reminding' me of the power of LOVE that was actually THE power of the universe. It seemed that I already knew this, but 'he' was just reminding me. We communicated for what I would have estimated to be about 20 minutes, then with no warning I was abruptly back on earth, in the same place I had been standing when the experience first happened. The astonishing thing was that it was obviously hours later as there was no-one in the room other than a sleeping body crashed on the couch."[106]

With this re-statement, a reminder of the existence of the other world and its power, Bronwen's mind was now truly focused. While the first trip to the clouds made her think, the second encounter cemented the knowledge of the reality of the spirit world into her very being.

Her thinking changed:

"The effect of these experiences on my life was profound. Overnight I had become intensely empathetic. I could feel any pain or suffering and sense of isolation of people passing me in the street. I had an overwhelming sense of needing to Do something... my search for what this something is, has dominated the rest of my entire life."[107]

Searching for Her Task

The "need to do something"; that is the faint recollection of a task, or a series of achievements, that she had signed up for before she was born.

At the time she wrote of her NDE, Bronwen have not yet discovered her mission. She had the sense of a goal ahead, but through the fog caused by her encapsulation on earth, the exact target is unknown.

In the book, *The Messengers*, Andre Luiz, the spirit who has dictated books to Chico Xavier, about his work in the spirit realm, learns about the importance of the missions that are meant to foster the spread of Spiritism on earth. Andre is curious about the success rate of the missions, he speaks with a knowledgeable person who explains the problems associated with their tasks, "Any constructive task has difficulties, barriers to be overcome. Very few workers have the willpower to fight the battles inherent in the challenge. An enormous percentage will balk at the first firewall they encounter and will retreat when the opportunities become threatening".[108]

"An enormous percentage", is a startling statement. This serves to disabuse ourselves of the belief of the smooth inevitable march to a higher plane. The war in the trenches is hard fought and is met with failure more often than success. One example of a failed mission by a spirit who is sent to earth is described by Octavio, a person that regretfully explains his unsuccessful mission to Andre:

"After having acquired great debts by committing crimes and injustices on Earth in former lifetimes, I eventually found my way to Nossa Lar and was helped by wonderful, tireless friends. In order to eventually return to Earth with a mission of service in the area of extrasensory communication, I underwent an intense thirty-year preparation. I was eager to pay off my debts and make something good out of myself. I could count on so much help! The Ministry of Communication gave me all the assistance and guidance it could; in addition, six friends also helped me immensely. Technicians from the Ministry of Assistance went with me to Earth and helped in my transition process. My life, exercising my well-developed mediumistic capabilities, was to make me part of a great team of spirit workers assigned to Brazil. Marriage was not in my program; not because the duties of a husband could be incompatible with those of a medium, but because, for my particular case, it was deemed advisable to exclude it".[109]

Octavio speaks about preparing for his mission for thirty years. The spirit world invested a great deal in Octavio, much more than is spent training people on earth for even the most complex tasks. Octavio goes on to describe that he had a wonderful mother who brought him up in the Spiritist doctrine, while his father was more materialistic, but still a good person. Octavio lost his mother at fifteen and his father re-married. His step-mother had three children and his father and step-mother together had three more. They were the six friends who had assisted him in the spirit world. Octavio was to nurture the small children after his father passed away. Octavio continues his story detailing how he treated his step-mother, who was always good to Octavio, "Not having anyone to turn to, she asked me for help again and again – and to my shame, I ignored her. Two years after my father's death, my stepmother, was diagnosed with a devastating skin illness and was confined to a clinic. By this time, my heartlessness had reached such a level that I was totally disgusted by her and the kids, and just walked away from it all – not realizing that I was abandoning my six best friends from Nosso Lar to an uncertain fate".[110]

Not only did Octavio fail individually, but he certainly must have adversely affected the mission of his six friends. This is an example of one of the failures recounted in *The Messengers*. Octavio is just one of many sent on missions, again in the book *The Messengers*, we learn from a trusted source:

"Since the very beginning of the spread of the Spiritist precepts on Earth, Nosso Lar has sent teams to the planet with the job of teaching moral values. Hundreds of workers leave here annually with the goal of helping others and making amends for their past faults. But this has not brought about the desired results. A few have achieved some success, but the majority of workers have failed altogether. We have provided assistance on numerous occasions, but have seen little success. Very few achieve their goal in the arduous realms of mediumship and spiritual teaching".[111]

Failures for individuals had many causes; pride, quest for material goods, bad marriages, sexual temptations and others factors that daily affect our lives and lead us to different choices. Not only do the reincarnated spirits have to contend with their own human weaknesses, but our materialistic society in general supplies hurdles to those who are actively striving to spread

Spiritism.

Bronwen is young and she is actively seeking her path in life. The spirit world didn't leave her without an added boost. She wrote about her heightened empathy and her ability to sense the emotional state of people who even just passed by on the street.

Somehow, someway signs and hints will arise to guide Bronwen on her path. Think about your own life, what coincidences, random encounters occurred to you. How did you marry the spouse you are with now? What sequences of events led you to your current vocation? All seemly innocent events brought on by chance. Don't be fooled. We are prodded into circumstances where we will have the opportunity to either pass or fail our challenge.

Bronwen will be given the same consideration. At some point in time in the not so distant future, the scene will be set to use her knowledge and newfound talents. She has the free-will to either accept or decline the invitation.

New Attitude toward Religion

With her sum of experiences, Bronwen sees the world differently. Her previous religious beliefs are now reset. She describes her metamorphosis.

"Yes. A complete change from being a disillusioned agnostic, to someone who sees the evidence of "God", of Love, everywhere and in everyone.

I remain disillusioned about the motives and practices of religion…. ALL religions!"[112]

One can well understand her point of view. History is replete with examples of religions that evolve toward their flock serving the priesthood, not the other way around.

The spirit world realizes the failures of humankind. Wherever wealth and power materializes the unscrupulous appear and take advantage of the situation.

When we sleep our spirits are able to travel. The spirit world uses this to bring selected people to lectures, so they may be reminded of their responsibilities.

A group of incarnate Catholics and Protestants are invited to hear a lecture, by the spirit Eusebio, to a mixed group of Catholics and Protestant, albeit a less dogmatic and more likely to be persuaded types of people.

Andre Luiz was surprised that the lecture was being held, he was told, "It's important to understand that Divine Protection shows no privileges. Heavenly grace is like the fruit that always results from earthly effort: wherever there is human cooperation, there too will be Divine support."[113]

Eusebio opens with what it meant to be a Christian in ancient times and reviewed the sacrifices they underwent. Next, Eusebio offers a challenge, "However, as heir to those nameless heroes who lived in affliction, of minds built up in the promises of Christ, what have you done with transforming hope, with unwavering trust? What have you done with the living faith that your forbearers acquired at the price of blood and tears?"[114]

Eusebio then delves into his opinion of exactly what these institutions of faith have actually accomplished:

"You have erected barriers against each other that are difficult to cross. Dogmatism poisons you; schism corrupts you. Narrow interpretations of the divine plan darken your mental horizons."

"What delirium has taken you as you involve yourselves in a mutual competition for the imaginary obtainment of divine privileges?"

"In times of old, Christ's disciples competed for opportunities to serve, whereas today, you look for every little opportunity to be served."[115]

After a devastating review of their faults, Eusebio arrives at his request, "Therefore, do not limit your demonstration of trust in the

Most High to the ceremonies of outward worship. Get rid of the indifference that chills your ornate cathedrals. Let us make ourselves each other's true brothers and sisters. Let us transform the church into the sweet home of the Christian family, whatever our interpretations might be."[116]

A plea for a less bureaucratic and more involved practice of their religious principles, and an appeal for less infighting and more focus on the fraternal family under Christ.

Whereas, the goal for Spiritists is the change the world, the request for the souls at the lecture is to return to their Christian roots and stop fighting each other. The Spirit world is not expecting the audience to change the world, but to outwardly demonstrate the teaching of Christ as revealed in the New Testament.

The Spirit world is first attempting to steer the ship of the large religious organizations back onto a truly fraternal course. Without this correction, the ability and the required openness to accept the Spiritist doctrine would be absent.

Hence, our failures to create a true and loving religious experience for many is apparent, and this is why the advent of Allan Kardec, who brought us the Doctrine of Spiritism and Chico Xavier, who psychographed more than four hundred books, has started.

Now, with our present technological and cultural state, the human race is in a state to receive the divine message. We are being notified via the documentation of daily revelations through NDEs spread across the globe that there is indeed a spirit world. A dimension in which we were created and live the vast majority of our lives.

Each of us has had previous lives. In which we had made mistakes and accumulated capabilities and new knowledge. All important to our next adventure on earth. As we mature and build a firm spiritual foundation, the spirit world expects us to respond. To acknowledge that we must create a balance between our material and spiritual life. That living without a goal, with no absolute morals is not a path to become a perfected spirit. Only by extending our hands and love to others, all others, without distinction can we ascend to our goal.

Chapter 13 – NDE - Ronnie - The boy who was ran over by a car

Ronnie was a young boy when his NDE occurred. Ordinarily, his accident would barely receive two paragraphs in the local paper. All of his neighbors would know of the tragedy which either killed or maimed the boy for life. His entire extended family would spend years caring for him.

None of this happened. Ronnie walked away from being run over by a car. Not just a glancing blow that spun him out of harm's way. A full-on encounter with the entire weight of an automobile driving over his body.

The Story

Ronnie's NDE story was gathered from the NDERF.org website. A fountain of compelling accounts, from different countries, different languages and cultures, all tales of a momentary intersection with a universe that is not ours.

Amongst a multitude of sightings into a parallel dimension. A dimension we can't perceive, but those who reside there can see us. We come from that other place, the "Other World" as the Druids called it. That is where we really live, not here, not in this dense domain, where our bodies grow and decay in a short span.

The Druids knew that we lived in temporary vessels. The Gauls would hurl themselves into battle, with their courage bolstered by their certainty that if they perished, they would return to fight another day in another body. Whereas, their undisciplined battle order fell time and time again to the well trained and ordered Romans, their bravery was never in doubt.

Little wonder that not only did Caesar take their territory and freedom, but in order to finally subjugate the unruly Gauls, he had to pursue and wipe out the Druids. Similar to what the Romans subsequently attempted with the Christians. Another dangerous religion that preached about a life beyond earth.

116

The Accident

Ronnie describes the events before his accident:

"I was sled riding down an alleyway that intersected with an avenue at the bottom. I could not stop before entering the avenue. I went out into the street and struck the front bumper of the white Cadillac with my head."[117]

A typical kid, seeking the thrill of sledding down a step road never realizing the danger which could await him below. As soon as Ronnie's head hit the front bumper, he left his body and became a spectator.

"That very moment I left myself and was out on the sidewalk. I was not standing on the ground, I was hovering. There was a girl my age standing on the ground next to me holding her head and screaming. I could hear her and I looked at her, she was very afraid of what she was seeing so I turned and looked in the direction she was looking. It was "Me" and I was in the process of about to be run over by the car. At that time a knowledge came to me that if I wanted any chance to live, I needed to slow the car down so when the tire went over me, the body had to be on its back. I knew somehow that if the car ran me over on my stomach, it would not survive. I did, I slowed the car down and was directing the car when to go over the body. I did get it to run over the body facing up and now I had to have the same thing happen with the back tire. The car being so low to the ground was making the body (my body) to roll over and over. Once it got near the rear tire I slowed down the car again so it ran over me facing up. It did, it ran me over facing up. Now the body was stuck behind the rear tire and a big clump of snow that was stuck to the car. I watched the car drag my body down the road until the intersected the next road. When the car hit the dip in the road, the body fell out. I remember being glad that it was over but the girl was still screaming. She screamed all the way through this experience. Because she was screaming a man came out of his house at the back door, looked towards us and looked in the direction the girl or we were looking. He saw my body and he ran over to it. The body was crawling, using only the left arm. I think it was trying to go home. Not sure."[118]

At the Hospital

Next, he was rushed to the hospital, He knew his entire body was full of blood from internal bleeding. When he reached the emergency room, the doctors told his mother that he had little chance to live. They could not operate because the internal bleeding was so profuse, that once he was opened he would immediately bleed to death. Ronnie was put on observation to determine if the flow of blood would diminish enough to allow the doctors inside to repair the damage.

A priest was called to give Ronnie his last rites and to make his mother and family comfortable in the knowledge that Ronnie would be taken care of in heaven.

"I remember things going on off and on. My whole family was there at the hospital. Six doctors were around me talking. My mother sent for a priest for my last rights. She did not know nor did any doctor know what I knew. I was going to be okay. When Father T arrived I tried to talk to him, but couldn't. I could only move my left arm and my head side to side. So I kept reaching out to him over and over again. Father T looked into my eyes and I shook my head no. We did not talk but we did. He looked again in my eyes with a smile as saying you been there and your going to be okay. I shook my head yes. He then told my mother he is going to be fine, that I did not need last rights. She insisted that he did. As he began the last right, we kept smiling at each other, like in conversation that we know but they don't."[119]

Father T was correct, His faith enabled him to realize the small boy laying on the bed, surrounded by doctors was going to pull through. Spirits who were also in the room, caring for Ronnie, giving him magnetic passes so his body could heal quickly, let the Reverend Father know that he would not lose one of his flock.

118

The doctors wanted to let Ronnie stabilize so they could operate. They left for the night, not really expecting to see Ronnie alive the next morning. Then Ronnie has a second close call the next day.

"The hospital kept a 24- hour vigil over me, taking vitals at times. The doctors told my mother if we can stabilize him we will operate. I knew that there would be no operation. In the early morning hours I fell asleep. The nurse panicked and started giving me oxygen calling for help. Little did she know, that blowing up my lungs with oxygen was piercing my lungs from the broken ribs. I could not fight her off nor the others that had answered her call for help. I could only move my left arm. So again I left my body and watched as they tried to help. Finally a male nurse said take the oxygen off and they did. I was fine."[120]

How did Ronnie know that supplying him with oxygen was the wrong procedure? He's just a boy. He knew because his guardian spirit was there with him, assessing the situation. Most probably, it was his guardian who notified the male nurse, via a mental suggestion, to come to the room and rectify the situation.

Later, the doctors came to Ronnie's bedside to assess the patient.

"In the morning the doctors began coming in one by one. They were discussing my condition and could not explain what happened to me with each other. But I knew. Finally the doctors went out and told my family, we can not explain it, but we can not find any blood in his cavity. He is stable and that they will continue watching me."[121]

How could Ronnie be healed and the blood that had filled his entire body cavity be re-absorbed? It was the work of a dedicated team of spirits, who came at the request of Ronnie's guardian spirit.

By utilizing magnetic passes, whereby Universal Fluid is directed at Ronnie's body, and transformed into Vital Fluid which

119

corresponds to his needs, the physical shell for Ronnie's spirit, was able to amass the resources required to heal itself.

Your body utilizes Vital Fluids, which is a modification of the Universal Fluids that make up everything in the Universe, these are altered to fit your own spirit and body. Vital Fluid can be thought as an energy force that maintains the various Force centers, otherwise known as Chakras, which are responsible for keeping all of your bodily functions in harmony. The more Vital Fluids you have, the healthier and more vitality you possess.

Ronnie fully recovered. His ribs healed and his flesh mended. He had no discernible injuries after his horrendous accident.

A Miracle?

Ronnie account of being struck by the car and surviving with no lasting injuries would easily be considered a miracle in many people's mind. The odds that a young child would escape free of future disabilities from front and back tires rolling over his body would be astronomical. Yes, with modern medicine many would survive, but to have no detectable bleeding in his body, even after the nurse gave him oxygen, is a true anomaly.

Therefore, was Ronnie's escape a miracle? According to Spiritism, no. A miracle is an act of God that is contrary to the laws of nature. An unexplainable incident. Yet, Spiritism states there are no events which do not follow the Natural Laws of God. Hence, all manifestations, no matter how improbable or completely impossible adhere to the Divine Laws.

While it may be a miracle to our eyes, the actual episode followed step by step a set of Divine Laws which rule the universe.

Whereas, we on earth are like the cargo cults of New Guinea. During World War II, the aborigines of New Guinea saw planes crash and sometimes misdirected parachute supplies land within their tribal boundaries. Having no notion of twentieth century technology, they believed the material goods dropped on them were manna from the gods. They devised symbolic copies of airplanes made out of bamboo and other plants from the jungle to notify the gods they were ready for more.

Our culture rejects anything we can't explain. Or, worse, we assign it a fancy name, to make it appear we comprehend a condition. But in reality, we are merely categorizing a mystery. One example of this hubris is the term "sleep paralysis". What is the definition of this condition? According to Wikipedia it is:

> **"Sleep paralysis** is a phenomenon in which a person, either falling asleep or awakening, temporarily experiences an inability to move, speak or react. It is a transitional state between wakefulness and sleep characterized by complete muscle atonia (muscle weakness). It is often accompanied by terrifying hallucinations (such as an intruder in the room) to which one is unable to react due to paralysis, and physical experiences (such as strong current running through the upper body). One hypothesis is that it results from disrupted REM sleep, which normally induces complete muscle atonia to prevent sleepers from acting out their dreams. Sleep paralysis has been linked to disorders such as narcolepsy, migraines, anxiety disorders, and obstructive sleep apnea; however, it can also occur in isolation."[122]

No mention of possession by spirits, other death experiences, after death experiences, no spiritual connotations whatsoever. As if the roots of our very existence, when humans lived closer to God and his messengers were all mere fragments of our collective imagination. The definition fails in its inability to precisely account for the multitude of people who swear they have been visited or talked to spirits. Anything to do with a world beyond our control is summed up in one word; hallucinations.

I confess, I too thought the same. I too dismissed any account I read or heard as the musings of weak minds. How could they be so stupid! Until the time that I, the know it all, experienced a series of events that could not be dismissed as a hallucination. No I didn't have a NDE or any type of conversation or sighting of a spirit, Jesus, or an all knowing God. Mine was simply being told of an upcoming incident. A foretelling that took more than twenty years to unfold that shook me off my pedestal and taught me that I know nothing and am nothing.

Suffice to say, that my wife was told of her future life with uncanny accuracy, including events that I, her husband, would experience. There were many things my wife told me. I was oblivious to all of them, putting each down to coincidence, but finally after the accumulation of proof, I was told exactly how I would lose my job, what the ramifications would be and who I would work for next, set me off on a discovery. A journey that I am still on. A quest to determine how could the future be told with certainty, when I the rational being, had absolute faith that we on earth were just random bits of organic material, that grew and died for no particular purpose.

Now I understand we are part of a fantastic universe of love. Not of leisure, but one of caring and hard work. Work that we require to perfect ourselves. And within our universe is a set of laws that we are guided by. Laws that for the most part are beyond our current understanding, but are rational nevertheless. As part of the structure of the Divine Laws, there exists a spiritual world with immense capability.

Capability that was responsible for Ronnie to be ran over by a car and not lose his life or become paralyzed.

What Probably Did Happen?

My interpretation of how Ronnie survived his ordeal is a little different that his perspective. Whereas Ronnie believed he slowed down the car, the greatest probability is that a guiding spirit, his guardian angel, vastly increased his ability to think and react.

When a person throws a punch at us, or an object is hurled in our direction, if we had not anticipated it, we would take about three quarters of a second to react.

The time it takes for a moving car to cross the same space from the front wheel to the back wheel is extremely fast. For an average car to stop at thirty-five miles per hour takes about 106 feet. A car traveling at 30 mph travels 44 feet every second. A 2015 Chevy Camaro is about 16 feet in length with a wheel base of 9 feet 4 inches. Therefore, at thirty miles per hour it would take approximately two tenths of a second to run over an object with the front and back tires.

Ronnie states that he maneuvered himself on his back, to protect his spine, before the first wheel hit him. Next, by the force of the forward motion of the car and the rotating tire, he spun around and again managed to perfectly land on his back once more just before the rear tire ran over him. A maneuver that a trained athlete wouldn't have a hope of performing.

What occurred was his guardian spirit fed his body the precise movements required. Aerial gymnastics in which Ronnie made a score of perfect 10's. Ronnie's perception was heightened to a degree of which we have no measure. He measured time in microseconds, seeing each one thousandth of a second as we perceive minutes. His guardian angel orchestrated his survival.

Not a miracle, but a demonstration of the power that surrounds us. A force of such immensity, that the time required to calculate the exact position for Ronnie's body at each moment in time, was done in an imperceptible interval. Then to communicate directly to Ronnie's conscious thoughts and have his body react according to plan is a task that our most powerful computers would surely fail.

Not a miracle, but a small gift to an innocent child and importantly to us a signpost. A marker, that points, thanks to Ronnie's description, onward to discovering for ourselves the wondrous world around us. Leading us to conclude that our knowledge of universal laws are woefully inadequate. We must acknowledge our immaturity and seek comprehension about the spirit world from unconventional sources. Sometimes, most certainly, we may be mistaken, while at other junctions, we may stumble upon the right track. We must get off the paved road of stifling convention and onto the path of our own discovery.

Ronnie's Experience in the Other World

When the ordeal of surviving the assault of the front and rear tires of the car was completed, Ronnie laid in the snow, watching the little girl crying and people rushing to his assistance, spirits talked to him:

"At that time and moment I was told to go back or come forward. I went over to my body, I did not walk I just floated like over. I was hovering over my body when again I was told its getting late make up your mind what your going to do. As I was looking down I said I am not going in there, the body was bleeding out it mouth ears and nose. I could see the pain it was in so I said " I am not going back in there." That is when I left the site. It sounded like some kind of machine turned on and I was in this very dark tunnel with a very tiny spot of light way way far in front of me. I could feel myself going forward towards the light. As I got closer to the light I noticed the light was brighter than any other light I saw in my life, but it did not hurt my eyes. The FEELING I had as I was getting closer was a feeling of love. Kind of being in your mothers arms but much much more."[123]

Ronnie made a logical decision. Why return to a banged up shell. Obviously damaged beyond repair. When your alternative is the home that you know you belong to. A place where you are lighter, healthier, smarter and faster. Where colors are more vivid and your senses are eight times stronger.

How do we know you are able to sense more? In the book, *Workers of the Life Eternal*, dictated by Andre Luiz and psychographed by Francisco (Chico) C. Xavier, a spirit comments on the capabilities of incarnates:

"Notwithstanding the progress of scientific investigation, ordinary humans can currently perceive only about one eight of the plane where they spend their existence. Sight and hearing, the two doors that could expand their intellectual research, continue to be greatly restricted. For instance, let us consider sunlight, which compress the basic colors that can be seen by corporeal eyes. We are only able to see colors that go from red to violet, and most people see nothing past the last five, which are blue, green, yellow, orange and red – they fail to detect indigo and violet. However, there are other colors in the spectrum that correspond to vibrations that the human eye is incapable of detecting. There are infrared and ultraviolet rays, which the human researcher is able to identify imperfectly but is unable to see visibly."[124]

Ronnie started making the journey home, via a gold road. Then he saw the person he had been missing for so many years.

"I walked some more and came upon a pair of steps. The steps were solid gold. I remember thinking that if I could take some of these steps back to my mother, everything would be fine. My mom was a widow for a long time and we suffered hardships along the way. On the side of the steps was a plaque and it read "flight ###", I can't remember the number but it was a three digit number. That is when I heard or noticed someone coming down the stairs. I ran a short distance away from the steps and knelled down in the fog so I would not be seen. As this person began to come down the steps, I could see his feet and ankles, then his legs. I felt now that I knew this person but wasn't sure who it was. As he came down the steps I could see his chest and his chest had a white corsage on it. I should of know at that point who he was but I didn't. My dad had a white corsage on his chest lying in his casket before we buried him. When his face came into view I saw that it was my daddy. I was six years old when he died. I got up and started to run towards the stairs yelling " Dad, Dad, oh Daddy I am sorry for what I have done." He smiled at me, I could see his gold tooth, and he stopped coming down the steps. He then said to me "it doesn't matter... as long as you are truly sorry for what you have done." And I replied " yes Dad I am really sorry." Then he said "well then, that's all you need. How about you coming to live with me for awhile?" I answered "yes, I would like that." He stretched out his hand for me to come and I did. He took me by the hand and turned around and we started walking up the steps. We took a few steps and we stopped. He sighed and ask me "what's wrong?" His head was down looking towards the ground, he never looked at me again, I answered, " I can't go with you, Mommy and Richie (my little brother) will cry."[125]

Once again, our loved ones, the people we miss so much in our lives are in the other world waiting. Waiting in a much better place than we. Our sorrow should be replaced with joy, knowing they finished their trial and are preparing for the next. A new adventure, comprising new courses of study combined with new events to push them on in their quest to become a better soul.

Ronnie's father knew his son had to go back, but he wanted Ronnie to know he was fine and to give Ronnie the faith required to finish his trials, his assigned classes.

The central reason we are here on this little planet in the middle of nowhere, is to better ourselves. Ronnie had just started his schooling in life, the spirit world wanted him to continue. His plan didn't have him returning so soon. Hence, the spirit realm patched him up, patted him on the head on sent him back.

Chapter 14 – NDE – Romy - The Car Accident which Triggered Perfect Recall

Romy was in a car, with her family, when their car went off the road and rolled down a mountain. Flipping over multiple times, the passengers were traveling at rapid speed down a ravine as if they were in a barrel. Then a voice spoke to Romy.

This account is taken from the Near Death Experience Research Foundation, NDERF.org, the complete report is on the site and the URL can be found in the Bibliography section of this book. It is a good idea to read my interpretation, then go back and read the full account. You may see the broader context and hopefully, spot other areas of interest to you.

The Reassuring Voice

As the car went over the edge and repeatedly flipped end to end, Romy heard a man's voice telling her that everything was going to be fine. While the car crashed into boulders and outcroppings on the side of the mountain, the voice told her to roll with the movement of the car. Romy describes what he felt next:

> "Feeling absolute peace, I let myself roll. The voice came as if from inside of my head but at the same time It wasn't "me". It was very comforting, stable and strong. I did not recognize the voice but I connected to it very deeply, and knew I could trust it with all my heart. As I was "rolling" with every tumble I suddenly wasn't in the car anymore.
>
> I experienced complete trust."[126]

Pictures began to appear in Romy's mind, as if she was seeing a movie frame by frame. Although, the film wasn't in perfect succession, some parts skipped ahead to different times of her life, with a narrow silver thread connecting one episode to another.

When she mentally inquired about a specific scene, the answer came to her immediately. She began to feel as if she was part of the spirit world.

"This unfolding of pictures and gaps developed and progressed continuously, presenting a constant delicate consequential line in perfect order, a chain of events, yet somehow they were all happening at once. The past the present and the future were all happening at once. It was inspiring to witness the order and sense that all these little pictures seemed to have in "the big picture". I felt a lot of compassion. I was all forgiven. In fact there was nothing to forgive."[127]

Without her explicit knowledge, Romy was in a space between physical and spiritual life, she began to do what high spirits are capable of, accessing whatever memory they desire.

The Memory Bank

Unbeknownst to us, we are delicate recording instruments. While we constantly struggle with our poor memories, forgetting tasks that we gave ourselves to do just moments ago. Car keys lost in a place where we just put them. Distractions cause us to completely blank out when and where we were supposed to meet a friend. All part of our normal routine. While we complain of being forgetful, in no fantasy universe do we expect perfect recall.

Except, there is another dimension and it's not a fantasy. It is actually the real world. This world we live in a dense shell. Our spirit is attached to our earthly spacesuit so it may be modified by our experiences during our classwork among the living. While our bodies' plays out the scenarios presented to us, our spirit records all.

These recordings can be used to investigate not only our actions, but the thoughts behind our deeds. Swedenborg, a famous Swedish medium in the 1700's wrote about what he witnessed during his time in the spirit world; one instance concerns people who have passed away and were being judged. As usual with unrepentant criminals, they refused to confess to the slightest infraction. Swedenborg tells how the high spirits presented evidence to the contrary.

> "To prevent them from believing they were blameless, everything was disclosed and drawn out of their own memory in sequence from the beginning of their life to the end."[128]

> Swedenborg goes on to say, "I have also heard that angels have seen and displayed from the memory of one individual everything he had thought one day after another over the course of a month, with never an error, recalled as though he himself were back in those very days."[129]

Three hundred years later, Romy speaks about, "a constant delicate consequential line in perfect order, a chain of events", which implies a detailed record. Romy goes on to describe the finite detail and the method to fully explore his past experiences.

> "As I was watching this linear unfolding of pictures, I realized that just by looking and focusing on a specific picture, "zooming in" on it, I could also "enter" that scene and then come back out of it, "zoom out" and return to my place of observation. I looked back at my childhood. I could enter pictures there.

> From each picture, moment or thought, there was always the possibility to access that light that separated between it and the next picture.

> I could also see all the thoughts I had all my life. Their "pictures" were as strong as the pictures that depicted action or words. I was amazed to see that our thoughts are that strong, so real. It looks like they were also threaded on a string of light."[130]

Swedenborg, an upper class and educated person, who lived in Sweden, but wrote in Latin and travelled extensively in Europe, at a time when questioning the tenets of Christianity was a dangerous business, saw the same phenomena as Romy in our postmodern world. A world where to believe in God and spirits is thought of

129

as a handicap to rational thinking.

Her near death experience caused Romy to reflect about what this flawless memory means.

"I could see my life was a perfect manifestation of just what it was, who I was. There was complete acceptance, even of those moments that I remembered as less pleasant. My life, all our lives were threaded with this light that filled the gap between each picture. In the moments that we are open to it, we connect with it. It is that simple. It is there always. "[131]

Watching the entire arc of her life, she saw the beauty of her assignments. She perceived the step by step progression of her spiritual awakening. She could feel the magnificence of the plan laid out for her. A plan in which, when she progresses from this life, she could look back and analyze each moment.

Swedenborg takes the same information and applies it to what Jesus told us:

"We may gather from these instances that we take our whole memory with us, and that nothing is so concealed in this world that it will not be made known after death, made known in public, according to the Lord's word, "Nothing is hidden that will not be uncovered, and nothing concealed that will not be known. So what you have said in darkness will be heard in the light, and what you have spoken in the ear will be proclaimed from the rooftops" (Luke 12:2-3)."[132]

Hence, the spirit world has presented us with a consistent message. From the New Testament, to Swedenborg in the 1700's, to Allan Kardec's *The Spirits Book*, in the 1800's, to Romy. Everything is archived, we are never unwatched, including our thoughts; all data is collected and stored for use at some later time.

The conclusion is clear; we can't just adjust our outer life and expect welcoming open arms upon our passing over. We must strive to adjust our thoughts and emotions. We don't bring actions with us, we only carry our memories and our current character.

Our moral fiber is the litmus test, not what we have done wrong previously, that we can pay off in time, it's our true self, our capacity to love and understand which is the ruler on what we are measured.

An Application of a Recording

The spirit world has at its fingertips every detail, every microsecond of our life. This mountain of information is used to help some spirits understand their past lives and how to improve themselves.

In the book, *Memoirs of a Suicide*, a group of recovering suicides are being brought forward in the lecture area to travel through their past lives to determine how they arrived at the life where they committed suicide. Each person, one by one, is seated in a contraption at the front of the class. There is a type of screen, but it is more like a hologram, where the memories of the person in the chair become real to the entire audience.

The first person to experience the interrogation is Amadeu Ferrari. He had cancer, and to pay for his treatments he embezzled money from the bank where he worked. His cancer was attacking his tongue and throat. His previous life appeared on the screen:

"Amadeu appeared to us, depicted by his own mind, in the year 1840 as a trafficker of black slaves from Angola to Brazil... He was from Portugal, which explained our affinity for him. By means of a series of voyages, he enriched himself with the abominable trade, not sparing any efforts in his vile ambition of returning to Portugal as a millionaire. He inflicted indescribable torment on the wretches as he rounded them up in their free homeland to make slaves of them and handed them over to other ignoble accomplices sharing the same deranged ambitions! In the truculence of inhumane conduct, he excelled in the mistreatment of his captives, ordering them to be flogged for the most insignificant wrong, or even for no wrong at all.... Once, on one of his plantations, he raped a black slave who was little more than a child. Her poor father was an elderly slave sixty-years of age. In a moment of supreme suffering

131

before the body of his child, who had chosen death to hide her shame, he had condemned Amadeu's vile act, accusing him of his daughter's suicide. In retaliation, Amadeu ordered cruel farm hands to burn the old slave's tongue with a red-hot iron until he collapsed in convulsions of agony."[133]

Fast forward, to Portugal, where Amadeu dies a rich man. He finds himself in the jungle surrounded by his old mistreated slaves. He spends years there tormented by all around him. Until one night, the old slave, Felicio, whom he had burned out his tongue, came up to him and said, "Come, master, get up... let's leave this place."[134] Felicio had forgiven him and came to free him from those who had not learned how to let go of the desire for revenge.

The instructor explains to the audience, that many of the slaves came from past lives as oppressors. Felicio, in his capacity working for the Roman Emperor Hadrian, committed many crimes and therefore paid his penance as a slave.

At the end of the interrogation, the instructor revealed a surprise for Amadeu:

"At a signal from Epaminodas (the instructor), a side door had silently opened and Felicio appeared, serene and grave, and walked towards his former master... Now in possession of his entire past, Amadeu looked at him in terror... Slowly and imperceptibly, Felicio transformed himself using the power of his will - which easily changes the configuration of the astral body - and let himself be seen in his role as Romulo Ferrari, Amadeu's father!"[135]

The machinations of the spirit world are a wonder to behold. When you read about the relationships that have been set up in the spirit world for us incarnates, it makes you think, who exactly is my mother and father, brothers and sisters, and other relations. We are all intertwined in the business of forgiveness, learning and salvation, we should look around and try to determine, who we are having trouble with right now, and what extra effort should we make to be at peace with that person.

132

What Romy Learned

As Romy was examining her life's record, she felt herself being drawn out of the blackness and traveling toward the mountain where the wrecked car and her body was laying still, almost lifeless. She realized she was between life and death, nearly ready to pass over.

Romy was able, for a finite instance, to feel what spirits feel, a sense of the love and joy that permeates the higher spheres.

"I recognized the light from meditation experiences I had, moments of insight, spiritual experiences, strong experiences of unconditional love, actually I realized this light was threaded inside every moment of my life and I have always, always known it and had access to it. I felt deep intimacy and powerful love, a great surrender, relief and joy. . From what I have seen our lives were threaded with this light, that fills the gap between each moment. At each moment, every situation, every thought, the light is always available to us. If we're aware that it's there we can remind ourselves to call on it. To connect to it.

I was now sitting near this light, near the source of it. I had never felt it so strongly. It was everything. Everything I have ever needed, everything I need or everything I might ever need in the future. Everything was in this light. It was warm. It had an immense healing and nourishing quality to it. It was pure, immense, powerful unconditional Love. I knew I could trust this light."[136]

The white Divine Light is what we are seeking. Romy instinctively knew she had a choice to make. Either stay on earth and complete her assignments or remain where she desired. Romy was wise enough to understand she still had more to learn. Lives are not to be wasted. They are meant to be used for the maximum gain. There is no limit on how much we can learn to be true spiritual beings.

The sight and warmth of the Divine Light changed Romy:

"I realized my purpose is to connect to this light I saw and share it with others. I felt a great urge to "put my hands on people" and transmit some of the light, especially in the first year after the experience. Whenever I want, I can close my eyes and connect to this experience, which immediately brings me to a place of trust and love."[137]

This is why the effort to allow our love to grow is worth the sacrifice. To feel an eternity of affinity with all that you love, outweighs the temporary material pleasures one could ever attain on earth.

Chapter 15 – Final Thoughts

Twelve experiences. Twelve different people. Various ages and a mixture of genders, of religions or lack thereof. Commonality only through shared communications with the other side. All came back with a sense that we are not here to live a brief life and then disappear forever back into molecules to feed the grass.

We are put on earth for a reason. We have a purpose and that purpose is not to accumulate material goods, but to gather love and understanding. To fully comprehend that a purposeful life is a life of service and caring. And to help us in our trek, we are given trials and tribulations to remind us what is useful and what is not.

We all should take comfort from the fact that we are not pushed out the door and left to wander alone. Just the opposite, we have an invisible coterie of well-wishers and guides, cheering us on and lending unseen helping hands at just the right moments.

All we have to do is demonstrate our willingness to take to heart the lessons assigned. Illustrate our capacity to remain caring and positive individuals amongst all circumstances. Serve as a light to others and assistance will be forthcoming.

For, indeed, you are here, on earth, this planet of atonement, where we are destined to accumulate knowledge in difficult terrain for as long as it takes to succeed. Hence, as we progress, our reincarnations will be more fruitful and worthwhile. Our stays more pleasant and rewarding, until one day, the need to take on a physical form has been removed. From that day on, we shall be a pure spirit. A spirit who is well-rounded, molded by the intense fire of hard trials, capable of undertaking any assignment for good by the Divine Intelligence.

Hopefully, the stories of love, joy, enlightenment and purpose will make an impact on your life. A tiny spark that there could be a higher meaning to your life. A small flame which gives you the strength to put in perspective the constant cry for self-aggrandizement in our present culture. For whatever luxury you believe will make your life complete on earth, is nothing compared to the reward a good life will return when you journey back to your real home, the spirit realm.

Chico Xavier, the great Brazilian medium told his friends what happened to him when we went to a cemetery to visit the grave of a recently deceased benefactor. The person had always been kind to Chico's foundation, giving money and food to help the poor. He was rich, but due to recent financial problems, he ended his own life. When Chico was at his grave, his spirit appeared and he told Chico, that Chico was the real millionaire, not he.

Therefore, live your life to the fullest, don't worry about the small obstacles in your path, for they are there because you agreed to place them about, so you could derive the wisdom you were seeking; to help you grow. To become a better soul.

You certainly don't have to live like a saint to ascend. You just need to balance yourself, to harmonize the balance between material necessities and your spiritual growth. Think about both and keep your life in perspective. Look down from the 50,000 foot level and see that problems are but transitory classes, from which you benefit. Be thankful for the opportunity to improve and try to impress the onlookers with your ability to care and your success will be assured.

Your Exploration Continues . . .

Learn more about Spiritism in my blog at:
http://www.nwspiritism.com.

To assist you in understanding more about Spiritism, I have
written four other books.

- The Case for Reincarnation – Your Path to Perfection
- Spiritism 101 – The Third Revelation
- 7 Tenets of Spiritism – How They Impact Your Daily
  life
- Explore Your Destiny – Since Your Life's Path is
  (mostly) Predetermined

In the next sections are the introductions to my books.

Join us on Facebook at: https://www.facebook.com/nwspiritism

Join our discussion group on Spiritism at:
https://www.facebook.com/groups/Spiritist/

Go to the source of Spiritism and read Allan Kardec's books. The
two I find most interesting are:

1. The Spirits Book

2. The Gospel According to Spiritism

Follow the life of the spirit Andre Luiz, psychographed by
Francisco C. Xavier as he rises to the celestial city of Nosso Lar
and he experiences different aspects of how the spirit realm loves
and guides us is one of the most satisfying reads in my life. There
are thirteen books in the series, only eleven in English at this time,
and I urge you to read all of them in order.

1. Nosso Lar

2. The Messengers

3. Missionaries of the Light

4. Workers of the Life Eternal

5. In the Greater World

6. Liberation

7. Between Heaven and Earth

8. In the Domains of Mediumship

9. Action and Reaction

10. Evolution in Two Worlds (not yet in English)

11. Mechanisms of Mediumship (not yet in English)

12. Sex and Destiny

13. And Life Goes On

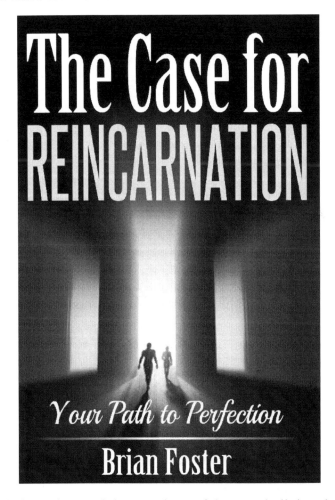

To fully understand the emotions of the people living through their NDEs and the actions of the spirit world in sending people back to earth, a review of how and why we travel through multiple lives is helpful.

You have lived multiple lives. At times you have been rich, poor, a servant and a slave. Maybe even a King or a Queen, at the least a member of the minor nobility.

Many famous people in the past have believed in reincarnation, such as Thomas Edison and Sir Arthur Conan Doyle. They both believed in the spirit world and made attempts to communicate with the world beyond.

There is a realm, a universe greater than ours and it is filled with intelligences that we can only wonder at. There are spirits around the earth who are actively helping and guiding us in our planning and during our actual incarnations.

You are interested in this book and in the topic because you know, in your heart that we are not merely chemical elements that dissolve with death. There must be something more, you know this, because of your own intuition, experiences and beliefs.

There are too many unexplained phenomena for there to be nothing after death. How do some people have past life memories? Why do children remember past lives and then lose the ability after a certain age? How can some people know the future? And more importantly, why do you have premonitions that come true? How could you know what could happen with such certainty?

Reincarnation is a tenet in many religions, such as Hinduism and Buddhism, and is frequently mentioned as parts of varied sects of Christianity and Judaism. It is the concept whereby we have a spirit, in which we retain our central personalities and memories, while in the spirit world, but lose our memories while in a physical form.

This book is here to answer your questions;

1. Why do we reincarnate?

2. How does the process work?

3. How many reincarnations must we have?

4. What memories do we retain from our previous lives?

5. Do we have control over our reincarnations?

6. Why must we suffer?

7. How may I insure my next life is better?

8. How may I progress to being a perfected spirit?

These questions are answered through the Doctrine of Spiritism. When, in the 1850's, the spirit world determine it was time for the human race to assimilate this knowledge in the hopes it would led us to understand the need to improve our spirituality and to achieve a better balance between our desire for material goods versus our desire to be a better person.

Explore what is your role and where you are in this journey. Determine your place and your future. Find out the reasons for your current tribulations and how to, not only survive your trials, but prosper through them.

Your journey in different bodies at different times in different circumstances is not without a purpose. You began as a primitive soul and through successive lives; you are being molded into a perfect spirit.

Dive deeper into all facets of reincarnation; my book is available at Amazon; *The Case for Reincarnation – Your Path to Perfection*

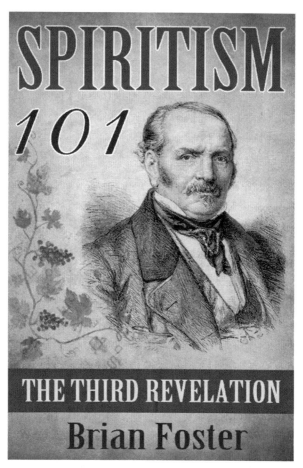

This short book is written as a review of the central concepts of the Doctrine of Spiritism.

Introduction

Something wonderful has happened. It occurred in the middle of the 1800's and it caught the attention of the world. It grew quickly in popularity, so fast that many in positions of power went on a crusade to stamp it out.

Why? Because it provided answers to questions that we all have been searching for. Questions that have been posed by philosophers since the beginning of time were asked and the results fully described.

Why such fear by the ruling religious classes? Because it explained the purpose for our life without dogma, without having to ask a priest or reverend for forgiveness. No special clothes to wear, no diet restrictions. No requirement for a specialized building or monthly stipends.

Why was it scorned? Because it didn't use the word "sin". It talked of spirits. It told us we could come back as either sex. And when it was asked about marriage, we were told that marriage is between two spirits, not two sexes.

We were told that a marriage should be the union of two spirits for as long as they work together in harmony. If not, then it wasn't the spirit world that stopped people from parting, it was our erroneous human convictions.

The organized Christian religions reacted strongly. They burned books and harassed those that knew and cherished the fact that the Third Revelation had occurred.

Like other messages of love, charity and fraternity before; this one was met with strong opposition. Ideas are hard to stamp out and this one is growing again. The world is re-awakening to Spiritism.

Learn what Spiritism is and how it can positively shape your life and happiness.

Available at Amazon Kindle and in paperback for - *Spiritism 101 – The Third Revelation*

What are the seven tenets? They are the essential fluid and air in which we swim, walk and run in our daily lives. The seven tenets explain why your life is the way it is and how by realizing the Divine Force that surrounds us is a force for love, you can surmount any obstacle and withstand any ill wind.

Not only survive but prosper. For that is why we are here on earth. To learn, to improve, and to gain experiences. To place in the bottom of your heart that love, understanding, caring and serving are the tools we should use to solve every situation.

Sounds easy but in practice it's difficult. Everyday life swirls constantly around us, as if we live in an eye of a hurricane, and every misstep buffets our emotions. Life is a constant hardship for many. We need to rise above the terrain and visualize the road ahead. From the ground it looks rough and rocky, but from on-high the path appears smooth and the destination closer.

I explore each of the seven tenets and how they have personally affected me and those around me. How they will alter your view of your life and change your outlook and priorities. Giving yourself the seven tenets could be the best present of your life.

The 7 Tenets of Spiritism:

1. We are Immortal Souls

2. God and Jesus Love Us

3. We have Multiple Lives

4. During our Lives We Pay for Past Debts and Accumulate New Experiences

5. We Live and Learn in Close Family Groups

6. Our Destiny is Mostly Predetermined

7. We are Assisted in our Lives by Unseen Spirit Forces

Available at Amazon Kindle in in paperback.

Explore Your Destiny – Since Your Life's Path is (mostly) Predetermined

Do you wonder if you have an important call with destiny? That you have been selected for something? A cause of a higher purpose?

Well you have been chosen and the why, when, where and how is the subject of this book.

Your life isn't one of just survival through the daily grind of life. The ups and downs of what you have been through are all for a purpose. Every key experience you have had, every calamity that befell you and each relationship that went south or well are part of your overall story. Each major event in your life has been planned.

Have you felt this could be true? Was there even a hint of recognition that certain events occurred for a purpose? And that you were seemingly on a train headed for some unknown destination and you couldn't get off?

This is because within your deepest thoughts, unconsciously, you recognize that you are part of a greater plan. A plan that has been drawn up with your improvement in mind.

There is an answer to your intuition and questions. The answer is wonderful and your part in the drama you are leading is fascinating. Once you realize the total environment in which you reside in, you will recognize that your life is not dreary, but a heart stopping adventure, a roller coaster ride that drives you forward into an unimaginable future.

Explore Your Destiny is divided into four sections. Each section supplies one more piece of the puzzle for you to place, so you can look at your life's arc with new insights.

1. Why – Why are we here and why must we live what we are living through right now? It's the age old expression, that we all say at one time or another, "Why me?" Well there is a reason and it will be explained to you.

2. When – In what period along your souls timeline is all of this happening? Yes, there is a greater context of your soul, which you may not be aware of. Knowing your relative position in the path to perfection will guide you to understanding your current life.

3. How – How does all of this occur? How does the entire process affect your destiny and actions? What are the rules of the game? Knowing the structure and comprehending the basic laws that direct your life provides you with a point of view that will put everything into perspective.

4. Where – Where is this world that plans our destiny? Are there good places to be and are there bad? Where does the earth fit into the logical structure? You will see

where the regions that you are striving to attain are and where you may be living in your not-to-distant future.

I hope that after reading this book you will have a new view of your life. A view that allows you to look at your circumstances from afar and identify the turning points in your personal destiny. I want you to be in that high level observation tower where you can dispassionately evaluate your life and calmly proceed through the good and bad times. Always keeping your eye on the ball of what your true goal really is – Your triumph in the Spirit and Physical worlds.

My book is available at Amazon; *Explore Your Destiny – Since Your Life's Path is (mostly) Predetermined.*

Author

Stay in touch with the author via:

Spiritist Blog: http://www.nwspiritism.com

Facebook: https://www.facebook.com/nwspiritism

Facebook group to discuss Spiritism: (please request to join)
https://www.facebook.com/groups/Spiritist/

Twitter: https://twitter.com/nwspiritism

If you liked *What Really Happens During Near Death Experiences*, According to Spiritism, please post a review at Amazon.

Copyright

Bibliography

Best of Sherlock. (2014, Dec. 20). *Best of Sherlock - Top 10 Quotes*. Retrieved from Best of Sherlock: http://www.bestofsherlock.com/top-10-sherlock-quotes.htm#impossible

Colorado State University. (2014, October 11). *CMG Garden Notes*. Retrieved from Colorado State University Extension classes: http://www.ext.colostate.edu/mg/gardennotes/231.html

Denis, L. (2012). *Life and Destiny.* Forgotten Books.

Dias, H. D. (2014, Dec. 23). *Seminário Apocalipse, Mitos e Verdades com Haroldo Dutra Dias_1ª parte*. Retrieved from YouTube: https://www.youtube.com/watch?v=4SU2b11IbMg

Dictionary.com. (2014, 03 02). *Dictionary Reference*. Retrieved from Dictionary.com: http://dictionary.reference.com/browse/didactic

E., N. (2014, Dec. 20). *Nicola E Friend Other*. Retrieved from NDERF.org: http://www.nderf.org/NDERF/NDE_Experiences/nicola_e_friend_other.htm

Ellis, M. (Dec., 26 2014). *blog.godreports*. Retrieved from God Reports: http://blog.godreports.com/2012/03/atheist-professors-near-death-experience-in-hell-left-him-changed/

G., D. (2014, August 1). *NDE Experiences - David G. ADC*. Retrieved from NDERF.org: http://www.nderf.org/NDERF/NDE_Experiences/david_g_adc.htm

Hooper, R. (2007, 2012). *Jesus, Buddha, Krishna & Lao Tzu.* New York: Bristol Park Books.

Kardec, A. (2006). *Heaven and Hell*. Brasilia (DF), Brasil: International Spiritist Council.

Kardec, A. (2008). *The Gospel According to Spiritism*. Brasilia (DF): International Spiritist Council.

Kardec, A. (2009). *Genesis - Miracles and Predictions according to Spiritism*. Brasilia (DF), Brasil: International Spiritist Council.

Kardec, A. (2010). *The Spirits Book*. Guildford, UK: White Crow Books.

Marshall, J. (2014, September 6). *My NDE*. Retrieved from NHNE Near Death: http://nhneneardeath.ning.com/profiles/blogs/my-nde-2

NDERF. (2014, Dec. 31). *WIlliam H NDE*. Retrieved from NDERF - Near Death Experience Research Foundation: http://www.nderf.org/NDERF/NDE_Experiences/william_ h_nde_7340.htm

NDERF. (2015, January 12). *Ronnie D NDE*. Retrieved from Near Death Experiences Research Foundation: http://www.nderf.org/NDERF/NDE_Experiences/ronnie_d _nde.htm

NDERF.org. (2015, Jan. 3). *Amy C Near Death Experience 4720*. Retrieved from nderf.org: http://www.nderf.org/NDERF/amy_c_nde_4720.htm

NDERF.org. (2015, Feb. 7). *Romy NDE*. Retrieved from NDERF.org: http://www.nderf.org/NDERF/NDE_Experiences/romy_nd e.htm

Near Death Experience Research Foundation. (2014, Dec. 13). *NDERF - Anna A*. Retrieved from NDERF: http://www.nderf.org/NDERF/NDE_Experiences/anna_a_n de.htm

Near Death Experience Research Foundation. (2014, June 28). *NDERF - Gail*. Retrieved from NDERF: http://www.nderf.org/NDERF/NDE_Archives/NDERF_ND Es.htm

Near Death Experience Research Foundation. (2015, 2 1). *bronwen C NDE*. Retrieved from NDERF.org: http://www.nderf.org/NDERF/NDE_Experiences/bronwen _c_nde.htm

Near Death Experiences Research Foundation . (2015, Jan. 01). *Sara A Probable NDE*. Retrieved from NDERF.org: http://www.nderf.org/NDERF/NDE_Experiences/sara_a_pr obable_nde.htm

Neto, G. L. (2013, June 15). *Remembering Chico Xavier and His Legacy*. Retrieved from YouTube: https://www.youtube.com/watch?v=wY5m3bk0AsY& list=TL01TkXUPh4dbuxLuFJq7Gmn-QZpLdKa5H

Pereira, Y. A. (2012). *Memoirs of a Suicide.* Brasilia (DF), Brasil: International Spiritist Council (EDICEI).

Spiritism. (n.d.). *Wikipedia - Spiritism*. Retrieved September 18, 2014, from Wikipedia: http://en.wikipedia.org/wiki/Spiritism

Steere, E. K. (2014, Oct. 6). *Research into Near Death Experiences Reveals Awareness May Continue even After the Brain Shutrs Down*. Retrieved from Daily Mail: http://www.dailymail.co.uk/health/article-2783030/Research-near-death-experiences-reveals-awareness-continue-brain-shut-down.html

Swedenborg, E. (1758). *Heaven and Hell.* Europe: A Publice Domain Book.

Swedenborg, E. (2011). *A Swedenborg Sampler.* West Chester, PA: Swedenborg Foundation Press.

Wikipedia. (2014, March 7). *Allan Kardec.* Retrieved from

Wikipedia: http://en.wikipedia.org/wiki/Allan_Kardec

Wikipedia. (2014, Dec. 24). *Bezerra de Menezes*. Retrieved from pt.Wikipedia (Portuguese): http://pt.wikipedia.org/wiki/Bezerra_de_Menezes

Wikipedia. (2014, August 21). *Camilo Castelo Branco*. Retrieved from Wikipedia: http://en.wikipedia.org/wiki/Camilo_Castelo_Branco

Wikipedia. (2014, March 7). *Chico Xavier*. Retrieved from Wikipedia: http://en.wikipedia.org/wiki/Chico_Xavier

Wikipedia. (2014, December 23). *Henry the Navigator*. Retrieved from Wikipedia: http://en.wikipedia.org/wiki/Henry_the_Navigator

Wikipedia. (2014, June 26). *Wikipedia - Emanuel Swedenborg*. Retrieved from Wikipedia: http://en.wikipedia.org/wiki/Emanuel_Swedenborg

Wikipedia. (2014, 11 22). *Wikipedia - Golden Rule*. Retrieved from Wikipedia: http://en.wikipedia.org/wiki/Golden_Rule

Wikipedia. (2015, January 12). *Sleep Paralysis*. Retrieved from Wikipedia: http://en.wikipedia.org/wiki/Sleep_paralysis

Wikipedia. (2015, Jan. 3). *Wikipedia - Fibromyalgia*. Retrieved from Wikipedia: http://en.wikipedia.org/wiki/Fibromyalgia

Wikipedia. (n.d.). *Wikipedia - Arthur Conan Doyle*. Retrieved September 20, 2014, from Wikipedia: http://en.wikipedia.org/wiki/Arthur_Conan_Doyle

Wikipedia. (n.d.). *Wikipedia - Carl Jung*. Retrieved September 20, 2014, from Wikipedia: http://en.wikipedia.org/wiki/Carl_Jung#Spirituality

Wikipedia. (n.d.). *Wikipedia - Carl Wickland*. Retrieved September 20, 2014, from Wikipedia: http://en.wikipedia.org/wiki/Carl_Wickland

Wikipedia. (n.d.). *Wikipedia - Subtle Body*. Retrieved September 20, 2014, from Wikipedia: http://en.wikipedia.org/wiki/Subtle_body

Wikipedia. (n.d.). *Wikipedia - Synchronicity*. Retrieved September 22, 2014, from Wikipedia: http://en.wikipedia.org/wiki/Synchronicity

Xavier, F. C. (2004). *In the Domain of Mediumship*. New York: Spiritist Alliance of Books, Inc.

Xavier, F. C. (2008). *The Messengers*. Philadelphia, PA: Allan Kardec Educational Society.

Xavier, F. C. (2008). *Workers of the Life Eternal*. Brasilia (DF) - Brazil: International Spiritist Council.

Xavier, F. C. (2009). *And Life Goes On*. Brasilia (DF), Brasil: International Spiritist Council.

Xavier, F. C. (2009). *In the Greater World*. Brasilia (DF), Brazil: International Spiritist Council.

Xavier, F. C. (2009). *Missionaries of the Light*. Brasilia (DF), Brazil: International Spiritist Council.

Xavier, F. C. (2010). *Action and Reaction*. Brasilia (DF), Brazil: International Spiritist Council.

Xavier, F. C. (2010). *Nosso Lar*. Brasilia - (DF), Brazil: International Spiritist Council.

Xavier, F. C. (2011). *Between Heaven and Earth*. Brasilia (DF), Brazil: International Spiritist Council.

Xavier, F. C. (2011). *In the Realms of Mediumship*. Brasilia (DF), Brazil: EDICEI.

Xavier, F. C. (2011). *On the Way to the Light*. Brasilia (DF), Brazil: International Spiritist Council.

Xavier, F. C. (2013). *Liberation*. Brasilia (DF), Brazil:

International Spiritist Council.

Xavier, F. C. (2013). *Sex and Destiny.* Miami, FL: EDICEI of
America.

[1] Steere, Tania and Smith, Emily Kent, Daily Mail UK, *"Research into Near Death Experiences Reveals Awareness May Continue even After the Brain Shutrs Down"*, n.d., http://www.dailymail.co.uk/health/article-2783030/Research-near-death-experiences-reveals-awareness-continue-brain-shut-down.html, (accessed February 15, 2015)

[2] Steere, Tania and Smith, Emily Kent, Daily Mail UK, *"Research into Near Death Experiences Reveals Awareness May Continue even After the Brain Shutrs Down"*, n.d., http://www.dailymail.co.uk/health/article-2783030/Research-near-death-experiences-reveals-awareness-continue-brain-shut-down.html, (accessed February 15, 2015)

[3] Steere, Tania and Smith, Emily Kent, Daily Mail UK, *"Research into Near Death Experiences Reveals Awareness May Continue even After the Brain Shutrs Down"*, n.d., http://www.dailymail.co.uk/health/article-2783030/Research-near-death-experiences-reveals-awareness-continue-brain-shut-down.html, (accessed February 15, 2015)

[4] Steere, Tania and Smith, Emily Kent, Daily Mail UK, *"Research into Near Death Experiences Reveals Awareness May Continue even After the Brain Shutrs Down"*, n.d., http://www.dailymail.co.uk/health/article-2783030/Research-near-death-experiences-reveals-awareness-continue-brain-shut-down.html, (accessed February 15, 2015)

[5]Steere, Tania and Smith, Emily Kent, Daily Mail UK, *"Research into Near Death Experiences Reveals Awareness May Continue even After the Brain Shutrs Down"*, n.d., http://www.dailymail.co.uk/health/article-2783030/Research-near-death-experiences-reveals-awareness-continue-brain-shut-down.html, (accessed February 15, 2015)

[6] www.nderf.org

[7] www.nderf.org

[8] www.nderf.org

[9] www.near-death.com/experiences/reincarnation02.html
[10] Kardec, Allan. The Spirits Book, White Crow Books
Questions 154,155, pp. 134-135
[11] Kardec, Allan. Heaven and Hell, EDICEI Cap. 2, items 7-8
[12] Xavier, Francisco C. Workers of the Life Eternal, EDICEI, p. 267
[13] NDERF.org, "My NDE", n.d.,
http://nhneneardeath.ning.com/profiles/blogs/my-nde-2, (accessed Sept. 6, 2014)
[14] NDERF.org, "My NDE", n.d.,
http://nhneneardeath.ning.com/profiles/blogs/my-nde-2, (accessed Sept. 6, 2014)
[15] Pereira, Y. A., Memoirs of a Suicide, EDICEI, p. 424
[16] Xavier, F.C., Missionaries of the Light, EDICEI, p. 179
[17] NDERF.org, "My NDE", n.d.,
http://nhneneardeath.ning.com/profiles/blogs/my-nde-2, (accessed Sept. 6, 2014)
[18] NDERF.org, "Michael Joseph NDE", n.d.,
http://www.nderf.org/NDERF/NDE_Experiences/michael_joseph_nde.htm, (accessed Aug. 8, 2014)
[19] NDERF.org, "Michael Joseph NDE", n.d.,
http://www.nderf.org/NDERF/NDE_Experiences/michael_joseph_nde.htm, (accessed Aug. 8, 2014)
[20] NDERF.org, "Michael Joseph NDE", n.d.,
http://www.nderf.org/NDERF/NDE_Experiences/michael_joseph_nde.htm, (accessed Aug. 8, 2014)
[21] NDERF.org, "Michael Joseph NDE", n.d.,
http://www.nderf.org/NDERF/NDE_Experiences/michael_joseph_nde.htm, (accessed Aug. 8, 2014)
[22] NDERF.org, "Michael Joseph NDE", n.d.,
http://www.nderf.org/NDERF/NDE_Experiences/michael_joseph_nde.htm, (accessed Aug. 8, 2014)
[23] Xavier, Francisco C., In the Realms of Mediumship, EDICEI, p. 9
[24] Ellis, M, blog.godreports, "Atheist Professor's near death experience in hell left him changed ", n.d.,
http://blog.godreports.com/2012/03/atheist-professors-near-death-

experience-in-hell-left-him-changed/, (accessed Dec. 26, 2014)

[25] Kardec, A., The Spirits Book, White Crow Books, Ques. 76, p. 96

[26] Kardec, A., The Spirits Book, White Crow Books, Ques. 115, pp. 112-113

[27] Ellis, M, blog.godreports, "Atheist Professor's near death experience in hell left him changed ", n.d., http://blog.godreports.com/2012/03/atheist-professors-near-death-experience-in-hell-left-him-changed/, (accessed Dec. 26, 2014)

[28] Ellis, M, blog.godreports, "Atheist Professor's near death experience in hell left him changed ", n.d., http://blog.godreports.com/2012/03/atheist-professors-near-death-experience-in-hell-left-him-changed/, (accessed Dec. 26, 2014)

[29] Xavier, F.C. Nosso Lar, EDICEI, p. 17

[30] Pereira, Y. A. Memoirs of a Suicide, EDICEI, p. 46

[31] Pereira, Y. A. Memoirs of a Suicide, EDICEI, p. 47

[32] Ellis, M, blog.godreports, "Atheist Professor's near death experience in hell left him changed ", n.d., http://blog.godreports.com/2012/03/atheist-professors-near-death-experience-in-hell-left-him-changed/, (accessed Dec. 26, 2014)

[33] Ellis, M, blog.godreports, "Atheist Professor's near death experience in hell left him changed ", n.d., http://blog.godreports.com/2012/03/atheist-professors-near-death-experience-in-hell-left-him-changed/, (accessed Dec. 26, 2014)

[34] Ellis, M, blog.godreports, "Atheist Professor's near death experience in hell left him changed ", n.d., http://blog.godreports.com/2012/03/atheist-professors-near-death-experience-in-hell-left-him-changed/, (accessed Dec. 26, 2014)

[35] Ellis, M, blog.godreports, "Atheist Professor's near death experience in hell left him changed ", n.d., http://blog.godreports.com/2012/03/atheist-professors-near-death-experience-in-hell-left-him-changed/, (accessed Dec. 26, 2014)

[36] NDERF, Individual NDE Experiences – 3669 Gail, n.d., http://www.nderf.org/NDERF/NDE_Archives/NDERF_NDEs.htm (accessed June 28, 2014)

[37] Ellis, M, blog.godreports, "Atheist Professor's near death

experience in hell left him changed ", n.d.,
http://blog.godreports.com/2012/03/atheist-professors-near-death-experience-in-hell-left-him-changed/, (accessed Dec. 26, 2014)
[38]Near Death Experience Research Foundation, "Nicola E Friend Other", n.d.,
http://www.nderf.org/NDERF/NDE_Experiences/nicola_e_friend_other.htm , (accessed Dec. 13, 2014)

[39] Near Death Experience Research Foundation, "Nicola E Friend Other", n.d.,
http://www.nderf.org/NDERF/NDE_Experiences/nicola_e_friend_other.htm , (accessed Dec. 13, 2014)
[40] Best of Sherlock, "The 10 Most Famous Quotations from the Sherlock Holmes Stories", n.d.,
http://www.bestofsherlock.com/top-10-sherlock-quotes.htm#impossible, (accessed Dec. 20, 2014)
[41] Xavier, Francisco C., "Workers of the Life Eternal", EDICEI, p. 365
[42] Hooper, Richard, "Jesus, Buddha, Krishna & Lao Tzu, Bristol Park Books, p. 138
[43] Hooper, Richard, "Jesus, Buddha, Krishna & Lao Tzu, Bristol Park Books, p. 139
[44] Near Death Experience Research Foundation, "Nicola E Friend Other", n.d.,
http://www.nderf.org/NDERF/NDE_Experiences/nicola_e_friend_other.htm , (accessed Dec. 13, 2014)
[45] Near Death Experience Research Foundation, "Nicola E Friend Other", n.d.,
http://www.nderf.org/NDERF/NDE_Experiences/nicola_e_friend_other.htm , (accessed Dec. 13, 2014)
[46] Near Death Experience Research Foundation, "Nicola E Friend Other", n.d.,
http://www.nderf.org/NDERF/NDE_Experiences/nicola_e_friend_other.htm , (accessed Dec. 13, 2014)
[47] Near Death Experience Research Foundation, "Nicola E Friend Other", n.d.,
http://www.nderf.org/NDERF/NDE_Experiences/nicola_e_friend_

other.htm , (accessed Dec. 13, 2014)

[48] Near Death Experience Research Foundation, "Nicola E Friend Other", n.d., http://www.nderf.org/NDERF/NDE_Experiences/nicola_e_friend_other.htm , (accessed Dec. 13, 2014)

[49] Near Death Experience Research Foundation, "Anna A NDE", n.d., http://www.nderf.org/NDERF/NDE_Experiences/anna_a_nde.htm, (accessed Dec. 13, 2014)

[50] Near Death Experience Research Foundation, "Anna A NDE", n.d., http://www.nderf.org/NDERF/NDE_Experiences/anna_a_nde.htm, (accessed Dec. 13, 2014)

[51] Near Death Experience Research Foundation, "Anna A NDE", n.d., http://www.nderf.org/NDERF/NDE_Experiences/anna_a_nde.htm, (accessed Dec. 13, 2014)

[52] Near Death Experience Research Foundation, "Anna A NDE", n.d., http://www.nderf.org/NDERF/NDE_Experiences/anna_a_nde.htm, (accessed Dec. 13, 2014)

[53] Near Death Experience Research Foundation, "Anna A NDE", n.d., http://www.nderf.org/NDERF/NDE_Experiences/anna_a_nde.htm, (accessed Dec. 13, 2014)

[54] Near Death Experience Research Foundation, "Anna A NDE", n.d., http://www.nderf.org/NDERF/NDE_Experiences/anna_a_nde.htm, (accessed Dec. 13, 2014)

[55] Near Death Experience Research Foundation, "Anna A NDE", n.d., http://www.nderf.org/NDERF/NDE_Experiences/anna_a_nde.htm, (accessed Dec. 13, 2014)

[56] Near Death Experience Research Foundation, "Anna A NDE", n.d., http://www.nderf.org/NDERF/NDE_Experiences/anna_a_nde.htm, (accessed Dec. 13, 2014)

[57] NDERF.org, "David G. - ADC", n.d., http://www.nderf.org/NDERF/NDE_Experiences/david_g_adc.htm , (accessed Aug. 1, 2014)

[58] NDERF.org, "David G. - ADC", n.d., http://www.nderf.org/NDERF/NDE_Experiences/david_g_adc.htm , (accessed Aug. 1, 2014)

[59] NDERF.org, "David G. - ADC", n.d., http://www.nderf.org/NDERF/NDE_Experiences/david_g_adc.htm , (accessed Aug. 1, 2014)

[60] NDERF.org, "David G. - ADC", n.d., http://www.nderf.org/NDERF/NDE_Experiences/david_g_adc.htm , (accessed Aug. 1, 2014)

[61] Near Death Experience Research Foundation, "William H NDE", n.d., http://www.nderf.org/NDERF/NDE_Experiences/william_h_nde_7340.htm, (accessed Dec. 31, 2014)

[62] Near Death Experience Research Foundation, "William H NDE", n.d., http://www.nderf.org/NDERF/NDE_Experiences/william_h_nde_7340.htm, (accessed Dec. 31, 2014)

[63] Near Death Experience Research Foundation, "William H NDE", n.d., http://www.nderf.org/NDERF/NDE_Experiences/william_h_nde_7340.htm, (accessed Dec. 31, 2014)

[64] Near Death Experience Research Foundation, "William H NDE", n.d., http://www.nderf.org/NDERF/NDE_Experiences/william_h_nde_7340.htm, (accessed Dec. 31, 2014)

[65] Near Death Experience Research Foundation, "William H NDE", n.d., http://www.nderf.org/NDERF/NDE_Experiences/william_h_nde_7340.htm, (accessed Dec. 31, 2014)

[66] Near Death Experience Research Foundation, "Sara A Probable", n.d., http://www.nderf.org/NDERF/NDE_Experiences/sara_a_probable_nde.htm, (accessed Jan. 1, 2015)

[67] Kardec, A., The Spirits Book, Guildford, UK, White Crow

Books, Chap. 4, ques. 175, p. 144

[68] Pereira, Y. A., Memoirs of a Suicide, EDICEI, p. 284

[69] Near Death Experience Research Foundation, "Sara A Probable", n.d., http://www.nderf.org/NDERF/NDE_Experiences/sara_a_probable_nde.htm, (accessed Jan. 1, 2015)

[70] Near Death Experience Research Foundation, "Sara A Probable", n.d., http://www.nderf.org/NDERF/NDE_Experiences/sara_a_probable_nde.htm, (accessed Jan. 1, 2015)

[71] XAVIER, Francisco C. In the Domain of Mediumship, Spiritist Alliance of Books, p. 35

[72] XAVIER, Francisco C. In the Domain of Mediumship, Spiritist Alliance of Books, p. 35

[73] Near Death Experience Research Foundation, "Sara A Probable", n.d., http://www.nderf.org/NDERF/NDE_Experiences/sara_a_probable_nde.htm, (accessed Jan. 1, 2015)

[74] Xavier, F.C. Missionaries of the Light, EDICEI, p. 327

[75] Xavier, F.C. Missionaries of the Light, EDICEI, p. 327

[76] Near Death Experience Research Foundation, "Sara A Probable", n.d., http://www.nderf.org/NDERF/NDE_Experiences/sara_a_probable_nde.htm, (accessed Jan. 1, 2015)

[77] Near Death Experience Research Foundation, "Sara A Probable", n.d., http://www.nderf.org/NDERF/NDE_Experiences/sara_a_probable_nde.htm, (accessed Jan. 1, 2015)

[78] Near Death Experience Research Foundation, "Sara A Probable", n.d., http://www.nderf.org/NDERF/NDE_Experiences/sara_a_probable_nde.htm, (accessed Jan. 1, 2015)

[79] Near Death Experience Research Foundation, "Sara A Probable", n.d., http://www.nderf.org/NDERF/NDE_Experiences/sara_a_probable_nde.htm, (accessed Jan. 1, 2015)

[80] Xavier, F.C. Missionaries of the Light, EDICEI, p. 310

[81] Near Death Experience Research Foundation, "Sara A Probable", n.d.,
http://www.nderf.org/NDERF/NDE_Experiences/sara_a_probable_nde.htm, (accessed Jan. 1, 2015)
[82] Near Death Experience Research Foundation, "Sara A Probable", n.d.,
http://www.nderf.org/NDERF/NDE_Experiences/sara_a_probable_nde.htm, (accessed Jan. 1, 2015)
[83] Xavier, F.C. Workers of the Life Eternal, EDICEI, p. 197
[84] Near Death Experience Research Foundation, "Amy C Near Death Experience", n.d.,
http://www.nderf.org/NDERF/amy_c_nde_4720.htm, (accessed Jan. 3, 2015)
[85] Wikipedia, "Fibromyalgia", n.d.,
http://en.wikipedia.org/wiki/Fibromyalgia, (accessed Jan. 3, 2015)
[86] Near Death Experience Research Foundation, "Amy C Near Death Experience", n.d.,
http://www.nderf.org/NDERF/amy_c_nde_4720.htm, (accessed Jan. 3, 2015)
[87] Near Death Experience Research Foundation, "Amy C Near Death Experience", n.d.,
http://www.nderf.org/NDERF/amy_c_nde_4720.htm, (accessed Jan. 3, 2015)
[88] Near Death Experience Research Foundation, "Amy C Near Death Experience", n.d.,
http://www.nderf.org/NDERF/amy_c_nde_4720.htm, (accessed Jan. 3, 2015)
[89] Near Death Experience Research Foundation, "Amy C Near Death Experience", n.d.,
http://www.nderf.org/NDERF/amy_c_nde_4720.htm, (accessed Jan. 3, 2015)
[90] Near Death Experience Research Foundation, "Amy C Near Death Experience", n.d.,
http://www.nderf.org/NDERF/amy_c_nde_4720.htm, (accessed Jan. 3, 2015)
[91] Near Death Experience Research Foundation, "Amy C Near Death Experience", n.d.,

http://www.nderf.org/NDERF/amy_c_nde_4720.htm, (accessed Jan. 3, 2015)

[92] Hooper, Richard, Jesus, Buddha, Krishna & Lao Tzu. New York: Bristol Park Books, pp. 138-139

[93] Near Death Experience Research Foundation, "Amy C Near Death Experience", n.d., http://www.nderf.org/NDERF/amy_c_nde_4720.htm, (accessed Jan. 3, 2015)

[94] Near Death Experience Research Foundation, "Amy C Near Death Experience", n.d., http://www.nderf.org/NDERF/amy_c_nde_4720.htm, (accessed Jan. 3, 2015)

[95] Near Death Experience Research Foundation, "Amy C Near Death Experience", n.d., http://www.nderf.org/NDERF/amy_c_nde_4720.htm, (accessed Jan. 3, 2015)

[96] Kardec, A., The Gospel According to Spiritism, EDICEI, pp. 37-38

[97] XAVIER, Francisco C. Between Heaven and Earth, EDICEI, p. 79

[98] Near Death Experience Research Foundation, "Amy C Near Death Experience", n.d., http://www.nderf.org/NDERF/amy_c_nde_4720.htm, (accessed Jan. 3, 2015)

[99] Near Death Experience Research Foundation, "Amy C Near Death Experience", n.d., http://www.nderf.org/NDERF/amy_c_nde_4720.htm, (accessed Jan. 3, 2015)

[100] Near Death Experience Research Foundation, "Amy C Near Death Experience", n.d., http://www.nderf.org/NDERF/amy_c_nde_4720.htm, (accessed Jan. 3, 2015)

[101] Near Death Experience Research Foundation, "Amy C Near Death Experience", n.d., http://www.nderf.org/NDERF/amy_c_nde_4720.htm, (accessed Jan. 3, 2015)

[102] Near Death Experience Research Foundation, "Amy C Near

Death Experience", n.d.,
http://www.nderf.org/NDERF/amy_c_nde_4720.htm, (accessed Jan. 3, 2015)

[103] Near Death Experience Research Foundation, "Amy C Near Death Experience", n.d.,
http://www.nderf.org/NDERF/amy_c_nde_4720.htm, (accessed Jan. 3, 2015)

[104] Near Death Experience Research Foundation, "Bronwen C Near Death Experience", n.d.,
http://www.nderf.org/NDERF/NDE_Experiences/bronwen_c_nde.htm, (accessed Feb. 1, 2015)

[105] Near Death Experience Research Foundation, "Bronwen C Near Death Experience", n.d.,
http://www.nderf.org/NDERF/NDE_Experiences/bronwen_c_nde.htm, (accessed Feb. 1, 2015)

[106] Near Death Experience Research Foundation, "Bronwen C Near Death Experience", n.d.,
http://www.nderf.org/NDERF/NDE_Experiences/bronwen_c_nde.htm, (accessed Feb. 1, 2015)

[107] Near Death Experience Research Foundation, "Bronwen C Near Death Experience", n.d.,
http://www.nderf.org/NDERF/NDE_Experiences/bronwen_c_nde.htm, (accessed Feb. 1, 2015)

[108] XAVIER, Francisco C. The Messengers, Allan Kardec Educational Society, p. 24

[109] XAVIER, Francisco C. The Messengers, Allan Kardec Educational Society, p. 40

[110] XAVIER, Francisco C. The Messengers, Allan Kardec Educational Society, p. 41

[111] XAVIER, Francisco C. The Messengers, Allan Kardec Educational Society, p. 35

112 Near Death Experience Research Foundation, "Bronwen C Near Death Experience", n.d.,
http://www.nderf.org/NDERF/NDE_Experiences/bronwen_c_nde.htm, (accessed Feb. 1, 2015)

[113] XAVIER, Francisco C. In the Greater World, EDICEI, p. 201

[114] XAVIER, Francisco C. In the Greater World, EDICEI, p. 204

[115] XAVIER, Francisco C. In the Greater World, EDICEI, p. 205

[116] XAVIER, Francisco C. In the Greater World, EDICEI, p. 208

[117] Near Death Experience Research Foundation, "Ronnie D NDE", n.d.,
http://www.nderf.org/NDERF/NDE_Experiences/ronnie_d_nde.htm (accessed Jan. 12, 2015)

[118] Near Death Experience Research Foundation, "Ronnie D NDE", n.d.,
http://www.nderf.org/NDERF/NDE_Experiences/ronnie_d_nde.htm (accessed Jan. 12, 2015)

[119] Near Death Experience Research Foundation, "Ronnie D NDE", n.d.,
http://www.nderf.org/NDERF/NDE_Experiences/ronnie_d_nde.htm (accessed Jan. 12, 2015)

[120] Near Death Experience Research Foundation, "Ronnie D NDE", n.d.,
http://www.nderf.org/NDERF/NDE_Experiences/ronnie_d_nde.htm (accessed Jan. 12, 2015)

[121] Near Death Experience Research Foundation, "Ronnie D NDE", n.d.,
http://www.nderf.org/NDERF/NDE_Experiences/ronnie_d_nde.htm (accessed Jan. 12, 2015)

[122] Wikipedia, "Sleep Paralysis", n.d.,
http://en.wikipedia.org/wiki/Sleep_paralysis (accessed Jan. 12, 2015)

[123] Near Death Experience Research Foundation, "Ronnie D NDE", n.d.,
http://www.nderf.org/NDERF/NDE_Experiences/ronnie_d_nde.htm (accessed Jan. 12, 2015)

[124] Xavier, F.C. Workers of the Life Eternal, EDICEI, p. 197

[125] Near Death Experience Research Foundation, "Ronnie D NDE", n.d.,
http://www.nderf.org/NDERF/NDE_Experiences/ronnie_d_nde.htm (accessed Jan. 12, 2015)

[126] Near Death Experience Research Foundation, "Romy Near Death Experience", n.d

http://www.nderf.org/NDERF/NDE_Experiences/romy_nde.htm,
(accessed Feb. 7, 2015)

[127] Near Death Experience Research Foundation, "Romy Near
Death Experience", n.d
http://www.nderf.org/NDERF/NDE_Experiences/romy_nde.htm,
(accessed Feb. 7, 2015)

[128] Swedenborg, E. A Swedenborg Sampler, Swedenborg
Foundation Press, p 34

[129] Swedenborg, E. A Swedenborg Sampler, Swedenborg
Foundation Press, p 36

[130] Near Death Experience Research Foundation, "Romy Near
Death Experience", n.d
http://www.nderf.org/NDERF/NDE_Experiences/romy_nde.htm,
(accessed Feb. 7, 2015)

[131] Near Death Experience Research Foundation, "Romy Near
Death Experience", n.d
http://www.nderf.org/NDERF/NDE_Experiences/romy_nde.htm,
(accessed Feb. 7, 2015)

[132] Swedenborg, E. A Swedenborg Sampler, Swedenborg
Foundation Press, p 36

[133] Pereira, Y. A., Memoirs of a Suicide, EDICEI, p. 506

[134] Pereira, Y. A., Memoirs of a Suicide, EDICEI, p. 509

[135] Pereira, Y. A., Memoirs of a Suicide, EDICEI, pp. 512-513

[136] Near Death Experience Research Foundation, "Romy Near
Death Experience", n.d
http://www.nderf.org/NDERF/NDE_Experiences/romy_nde.htm,
(accessed Feb. 7, 2015)

[137] Near Death Experience Research Foundation, "Romy Near
Death Experience", n.d
http://www.nderf.org/NDERF/NDE_Experiences/romy_nde.htm,
(accessed Feb. 7, 2015)

Made in the USA
Lexington, KY
30 October 2015